AF284285

Günther Kunstmann

… with JESUS on patrol!

**Experiences from more than 40 years
of police service**

and why prayer has to do with the police!

To make you smile ☺ and think about!

Bibliographic information of the „Deutsche Nationalbibliothek“:
The German National Library lists this publication in the „Deutsche
Nationalbibliografie“; Detailed bibliographic data are available on the
Internet via "http://dnb.dnb.de/".

The biblical quotations are unless otherwise stated,
taken from the New Living Translation.
Bold type or annotations in brackets is an accentuation of the author.

Title of the original version:
"mit Jesus auf Streife" © 2018
Translation into English:
Maria Deutsch / Bamberg / Germany
Günther Kunstmann
read correction: some friends in England

Cover photography: Günther Kunstmann

Editor: Andra Kunstmann, Bamberg / Germany

Production and publishing company:
BoD – Books on Demand
Norderstedt

ISBN: 9783753420783

Dedication

I dedicate this book to all colleagues who risk their lives and their health day and night to master one of the most difficult tasks of our society - the police profession!

Sure, there are lots of other jobs in which men and women master similar challenges and do deserve great appreciation and thanks – but I have been and still am a police man with all my heart, so my dedication is aimed to this profession.

When others are at home with their families and friends, celebrating, sleeping, relaxing, pursuing their hobbies, enjoying Christmas Eve, New Year's Eve, public holidays, and many other good times, police officers are on duty to serve, protect, and serve people conscientiously, with motivation and dedication. To take care of their needs and helplessness and to find the best possible solution.

Despite the hostility, insults, resistance and injuries, they never give up but accept the challenge again and again and go on patrol which is admirable.

Thank you for all the years serving together, having fellowship, mastering difficult police operations together, thank you for your backing in dangerous situations, your advice and help – not only in official affairs.

You are awesome!

Personal foreword

In this book you will read about ...

... my life, my life as a convinced Christian being a police officer.

... my partly curious experiences on the streets during lots of police operations.

... my practical experience and – connected to that – a more sensible perception, my spiritual development and my growing enthusiasm about my faith in Jesus Christ.

... the connections between police investigations, dangerous situations and principles of the biblical faith.

... the changing power of prayer and the practical impact on the investigative processes, social influences and the lives of people.

These are real life stories, some are hard to imagine or sound unlikely. Funny, strange, unbelievable, not scientifically provable or discussed. Sad, depressing, but also joyful when you see the positive change in people's lives.

I have seen ups and downs of people, looked into psychological abysses and terrible fates. From the little innocent child to the brutal professional gangster, I got to know them all. I have seen things you will never find in a crime thriller, but still happen again and again.

I was on the streets most of my time in the police. There I felt comfortable, it was my place. Very close to the action, if possible the first one to arrive at the scene. Out there, life was pulsing with all its positive and negative aspects.
Right there I belonged as a Christian - to the "front line", where I or where prayer was needed.

Official background:

Of course, I can't always give you all the details here, because people are still alive and nobody has to know about official procedures (even though they might be interesting...). I can´t tell you about many stories because they are too terrible. There are pictures which are burnt into my soul and took me weeks to get over, but I could not forget what I had seen. Only through prayer and conversations with my wife these experiences lost their fright, but they are still present today.

I have changed names, locations, radio paging names and other details to guarantee the best anonymity and data protection, but still to be able to tell the stories excitingly, vividly and truthfully.
I am writing about my experiences as I can remember them. Unfortunately I have not kept a diary during my time of service. I should have done it. But I can still remember lots of things and details of all these times.

In November 2017 I retired from over 40 years of police service and I thank God for the things I got to experience. It is not self-evident, especially if you get a heavy brain hemorrhage shortly before the retirement and the doctors give you two more days to live. Also here, the power of prayer was the reason I survived, experienced two miracles, I could even go back to my police work after a long period of illness (unfortunately only office work) and was then officially retired at the age of 60.
You can read about this part of my life in my first book called "Acts 29". More details are found at the end of this book.

I certainly didn't do everything right, hadn't been prepared for many scenarios in training (1976 – 1979) even though it was very good. Over the years I suddenly was confronted with a certain situation that I had never experienced before, I had no idea what to do, but I had to find a good solution nevertheless. I was often forced to improvise or find an unusual way to manage that situation. Always according to the law and to my best judgement. Afterwards, I thought very often to myself: "How on earth did you come upon that?!"

I was not perfect (and unfortunately still I´m not!), I have made mistakes, treated colleagues the wrong way and made them angry or hurt them. At this point I want to say again:

"I´m sorry, I apologize and please forgive me!"

For many years there were only men in the police, the girls came years later. They changed the police climate, broke the male domain, made many areas easier for us boys and some more difficult. Many female colleagues were absolutely super, even in difficult missions, others were not.

For the sake of simplicity, I will only write about "colleagues" or "policemen" in the book, even if female colleagues were involved.
Please excuse me for that.

If necessary, I will mention the fact that a police officer was female.

This way of phrasing does not represent a degradation of her person or femininity on my part, it is also not a "Macho Act", it is simply easier to write and read.
For me, terms such as colleague, citizen, policeman, etc. are gender-neutral, even if it is partly seen differently. But as we all know, this is a matter of discussion.

Personal background:

Together with my wife Andra I´m leading an independent charismatic church in Bamberg / Germany,
the "Jesus Gemeinde Bamberg".   (www.jesus-gemeinde.de)

For more than 25 years we have been the pastors and leaders of this church and during all the years I have experienced the support and the carrying prayers of brothers and sisters in faith. Also my parents and physical sisters have accompanied me in prayer over all these years.
Thank you so much for that – you are true heroes.

Andra has been and is my support, my counselor, motivator, my brake when I was / I´m too fast, the acceleration, when I was / I´m too slow, the shoulder I could cry on, and so much more. Without her, my time on the streets as a policeman would have been way more difficult.

She is a God-given present to my life, a faithful companion at my side.
Blessed is the man with such a woman at his side!
And that is me!

In many preachings I have told many examples from my everyday life as a police officer, I have asked my church for support with prayer for many cases, with partly, prompt and resounding successes. But while preserving the secrecy of the police service! Claro (= spanish/portugues and means "of course").

I am also writing this book because I´m repeatedly being asked about my experiences in the police, especially by young people.

Because in many conversations with colleagues and pastors of other churches both in Germany and abroad I realized that they still know very little about the connection between society, police, church, prayer and the spiritual authority. I hope I can brighten up this topic a little, heat it up and motivate it to be copied.

And "last but not least" I wrote this book out of thankfulness, because Jesus accompanied, guided and protected me throughout my entire police time.

HE was comforting me whenever my soul was not well anymore. HE was rejoicing with me about official success, HE forgave me when I had done wrong or when I was too gutless or comfortable to tell others about HIM.

Thank you Jesus for a lot of fun, success and countless encounters with people in my time as a Cop.

Jesus – it is so good to have YOU in life.

Jesus is worthy of all thanks and praise!

It´s all about HIM, not about me, not about how good I was as a Cop. Jesus is the Saviour, Healer, Comforter and Rescuer, not me.
I was able to help, comfort and help many people in their great needs - through Jesus.
Plenty of uniform shirts had to be put in the laundry because both - men and women wept on my shoulder, in my arms crying out the pain of the soul - out of the body. But it was worth washing the shirts.

This is not a teaching book "How to become a good Cop or a good Christian", it is simply a ramble through my life as a "Jesus freak" working for in the police!

with one word:

with Jesus on police patrol!

Stop!
Attention, please!
this is the police speaking!
(or Günther ☺)

Foreword by Raul N. Reyes / Argentina

You have in your hands what I call a truly challenging and revealing book. It shows us how, as Christians, we can enter into the handling of everyday life and experience testimonies. The book also clearly shows that Christ is not only concerned with doing this in the four walls of the church, but also with extending the dominion and authority given to us by our Lord Jesus Christ to the realm of everyday life. Where "being a Christian" becomes much more than just a word and the power to change into a "lifestyle" becomes clear under the guidance and conception of the Holy Spirit.

In this case it is a Holy Spirit-filled Christian policeman from the city of Bamberg / Germany who understood the role of Christians in administering the power given by Jesus Christ to the Church, the knowledge and revelation of the spiritual world, and put it into practice, not only to bring security to his city, but also to open the heaven to bring peace and blessings to his "City of God".

In this book, the pastor and policeman Günther Kunstmann writes in an entertaining, practical and testimonial manner what we can do in every area of our lives and actions if we believe and implement what the Apostle Paul expresses in **Ephesians 6 : 12:**

> *„For we are not fighting*
> *against flesh-and-blood enemies,*
> *but against evil rulers*
> *and authorities of the unseen world,*
> *against mighty powers in this dark world,*
> *and against evil spirits in the heavenly places."*

This book is not only for believers in Jesus Christ, but for all who ask daily what I can do to bring a change in my work, family or profession. I assure that you will not be the same after reading this book. Once you have read this book "with Jesus on patrol", bow your knees and ask Jesus to transform your life from a cold, sluggish and religious faith into a faith of action and conquer for yourself personally the word from **Mark 16 : 17:**

"And these signs will follow those who believe..."

I particularly recommend this book to my police colleagues who patrolling and serving in the different cities of the world and often ask themselves: "What can we do to bring about this change?"

I believe with all my heart, also as a pastor and police officer (after 31 years of service, now retired), that we, Christians filled with the Holy Spirit, should undo the works of evil and change our society with the power of the Gospel of Jesus Christ!

Apostle Raul Nicolas Reyes
Police Social Psychologist
Sub Comisario (retd)
Police of the Province Buenos Aires
Argentina

Foreword by Fred Lambert / Austria

I just finished reading "with Jesus on patrol" by my good friend Günther Kunstmann. What a fun book! What an encouraging book! What a powerful book! This book is a great book for both believers, seekers and nonbelievers alike! Günther's 41 + years as a police officer in Bamberg were filled with danger, suspense, and sometimes sorrow. But they were also filled with adventure, heroism, humor and hope. His conversational and humorous writing style will put a smile on your face ☺ and warm your heart. The stories he shares are entertaining but they will also encourage you and teach you some of life's most important lessons. Forgiveness, compassion and understanding fill these pages because they fill the heart of the man who wrote them.

My wife Judy and I have been friends with Günther and his wife Andra for a number of years. We are also colleagues and comrades in Christian ministry. Judy and I are Pastors of the "Freie Christengemeinde" in Wels / Austria and Directors of "Rhema Bible Training College Austria", which is the largest free church Bible Institute in Austria. Günther and Andra are Pastors of a wonderful church in Bamberg called "Jesus Gemeinde". We met years ago at a conference in Germany and since then a genuine and meaningful friendship has developed over the years. Their faith is not religious, stuffy or boring – it is authentic, living and powerful.

Günther was raised in a Christian family and it was always his upmost desire to live for Jesus and do what God wanted him to do. This might surprise some people but this heartfelt desire to do God's will also led him to choose a career in law enforcement. The decision for this path wasn't easy for many reasons. Back then, when he decided to become a police officer, the times were turbulent and many people in his age group were anti-establishment and anti-police. The police were ridiculed, mocked and criticized by the anarchist, free love, flower power, hippie generation!

Another challenge was that some Christians believed that law enforcement was a completely unacceptable career for a believer. They somehow thought that Christians should be pacifists. According to their opinion, a Christian shouldn't carry a gun or ever use one and since police have to do this, this couldn't be the right career for a believer. These thoughts concerned Günther, so he took the issue to God in prayer. God revealed to him from the Bible that law enforcement is indeed a call and career that God himself established for the good of humanity. In chapter 13 of the letter to the Romans, Günther saw that the Apostle Paul refers to the agents of law enforcement as, "God's servants." Various other scriptures came to light and after seeing these things, Günther made the decision that eventually provided the subject matter for this book.

He writes:

"The decision had matured, been prayed through, confirmed by God and put into action thanks to the loving support of my parents. I was with the "Bavarian Cop's" ! I knew I was right. I belong to the "Servant of God", an instrument of God".

He unashamedly lived his faith in Christ as a police officer in Bamberg, which led to some very interesting and unique experiences. You'll read stories like "U-903 on combat patrol" or "The Naked Nun" and be both entertained and amazed by the humour of man and the wisdom of God. You'll read about the power of prayer and how the prayer stopped a series of accidents. Better yet, you'll learn how you can apply the same principles and power of prayer in your life to bring change and blessing to you, your family and your city.

His career as police officer also helped him better understand what it means to operate in the authority of Jesus Christ. Günther explains that the police have been entrusted with authority to enforce the laws of the land. They have been given training, a uniform, equipment and weapons to fulfill their duties. In much the same way, Jesus Christ has given us authority, training, armour and weapons to act in His Name on earth. We are called to enforce His victory in this world. We are called to break the power of the enemy, destroy the works of the devil, heal the sick and set the captives free in the mighty Name of Jesus. Günther writes:

"Jesus authorized us to do things in his name. To speak to the problems and to the diseases to change it."

This book is filled with true stories about how this worked for him on the job!

One of my favourite aspects of this book is the authenticity with which it is written. He doesn't hide his mistakes or the fears he had at first. He doesn't try to make himself into the hero of the story. He tells things like they really were in his own words and makes it clear that God has been his helper all along.

His motive in this book is not to impress and astonish the reader with lots of great stories nor is it first and foremost to defend his choice of career. His motive is to help people see that God will help them in every area of their lives, no matter who they are or what career they have chosen. God protects, delivers, heals, answers prayer, provides, grants wisdom and, most importantly of all, saves all those who call upon His name!

You're going to enjoy this book. I believe that when you reach the end, you'll be encouraged, inspired and ready to stand up and enforce the victory of Jesus Christ in your own life and in your own world!

God bless you!

Pastor Fred Lambert
Freie Christengemeinde Wels / Austria

Table of contents

Serious gangster on the run!

„Here is the operations centre to all patrol cars:

Escaped felon has entrenched himself in a hut at the foot of the "Kogelberg" (= name of a mountain), south side.
He is heavily armed and makes ruthless use of the gun. He has announced that he will not be arrested again, but that he would rather die in a gunfire wth the police. All patrols to the "Kogelberg", surround the area, more info will come soon! Pay attention to self-securing!
Patrols with bullet vests and heavy weapons come from the department!"

The radio call from the operations centre interrupted the pleasant talk I had with my colleague. So far there hadn't been much activity on the patrol that day. The usual checks, traffic controls, etc.

All of a sudden, we were in a dicey situation. We were not far away from the "Kogelberg". As a young cop I had never experienced anything like this before.
Okay, in the training we learned self-safety, handling the pistol and the gun. But now we only had the pistols with us.
Walther PP (weapon manufacturer and type), Caliber 6.35, also called "knocker of the police". You could hit the gangster, without visible success and that the hit showed any reaction.
That was something but not an adequate arming.

There were only a few bullet vests at the department. The personal vests for each police officer came years later. The ones in the department were forever heavy and "steel plate vests," you would almost bow down unpractical – literally – whenever you had to wear them. But better than nothing and better than dead.

The rifles "Fabrique Nationale (FN) G 3" and ammunition „caliber 7.62" were also stored in the department and we were trained on them.

Because they were not needed during a normal patrol, everything had to be packed up and brought to the scene in a case like this.

Whether we already had the MP 5 (Heckler & Koch, 9 mm) tommy gun as standard at that time, I don't know anymore.

We confirmed the operation by radio and started to drive to the location.

It became quiet in the patrol car, everyone was lost in his own thoughts. "What would happen? What awaits us? Will we get home safe? Will we arrest the guy?"

Questions after questions, but no answers. It was awful and caused pretty much of stress, especially for a young policeman like me. My goodness! The police academy just finished and then immediately into the full action.

My "bear trainer" ("Bärentreiber") said almost nothing, except: "Stay calm, we'll get it."

Oh, you don't know what a "bear trainer" is? Come on!
Claro – it is an old bavarian police slang.

The "Bärentreiber" – "bear trainer" was an experienced colleague, a veteran, who took a "boy" under his wings and helped him to learn police practice after his mainly theoretical training.

He was briefing the young one in the own police district, explained the official requirements and special features, knew where to find the best and cheapest snacks on patrol, where the crooks went and much more.

He was indispensable for settling into a department.

Today the training is strongly practice-oriented right from the beginning, with various internships. In class you also learn a lot for the practice.

We didn't have it that way back then.

And for this you have a practical guide. That´s what I´m saying – a "Bärentreiber"! A bear driver!

The tone and the expressions in the early Seventies were still a bit rough, partially they still came from the vocabulary from the "German Wehrmacht" (name of the German army until the end of the World War II) or even earlier, without immediately glorifying or associating any stupid Nazi ideas with it.

The term "Bärentreiber" was just like that and is still used today. It was/is not offensive or derogatory. On the contrary, it was a distinction and honour, a sign of trust from the chief, when someone was "appointed" to be a "bear trainer" for a young colleague. And we looked respectfully up to him. He knew everything (ok - almost), was experienced, could handle any situation and was like a father.

There has also been times for a bawl, a clout or other rebukes. But that was ok, you wanted to learn and one day be "adored" by a "police - boy". You were not allowed to be a mimos (a sissy) or too sensitive, then you were unsuitable for this job.

The training in the Bavarian riot police of the 60s and 70s was partly semi-military. We learned to throw hand grenades, to shoot with the old German machine gun MG 42 (WW II!). You`ll never know!

My old colleagues can still sing that famous song about it.

"A song! Everybody together! Two, Three, Four! O - oh, beautiful Westerwald (a large wood in Germany)..."

Enough of the memories now, let's get back to the story.

More and more patrols answered via radio, the loop around Kogelberg tightened and tightened and consequently around the felon. He was pushed more and more into the narrowness and probably more and more into the final despair. There were no special forces yet, no negotiating group, the men of the patrol had to solve that problem.

We were all lost in thoughts when I suddenly realized: Well, I could pray now! I mean, I was a Christian!

And immediately, a Bible verse came into my mind:

> *„Then call on me when you are in trouble,*
> *and I will rescue you,*
> *and you will give me glory."*
> Psalm 50 : 15

Bam! Awesome! It immediately touched me and I knew: God had spoken to me.

Out of the blue (somehow fitting or?) this Bible verse had come to my mind.

And before that, I had not even thought about doing the most normal and the most obvious thing:

PRAYER!

Mamma Mia! I really was a fool!

So I directly started to pray in my mind. Honestly - I did not dare to pray loudly. I did not want to show any weakness in front of my bear trainer. (So I thought at that time that others would think something like that about me).

> "God, please intervene and make sure
> that we don´t have to shoot or fight.
> Let him surrender!
> Amen."

I didn´t know how to pray in a better way at that time.

That was really a bold prayer for me and almost impossible. The felon had announced that he would not give up – he will shoot. And there comes such a young police boy and thinks that prayer can change a situation like that.

And behold – it does help – in fact, very good.

A short time later our operations centre came back via radio: **"Here Mark 2, here Mark 2! Abort approach, mission finished! The felon just surrendered and was arrested without resistance. Variety of sharp weapons ensured"**.

I was amazed! So fast and not really expected. God had surprised me and shown me that it would be better to trust HIM. That anything is possible for HIM. He had done it although I had not really believed in my own prayer. (shame on me)

And the end of the story?
- situation clarified
- nobody hurt
- the gangster arrested again and locked up safely
- the Word of God had proved to be true
- God stands by HIS word
- we can and should take HIM at his word
- my faith and trust was strengthened
- one of the first experiences with police and prayer
- everything ok!

By the way – I would like to mention something about the Word of God:
On the previous page I cited Psalm 50 : 15. This verse does not only speak about help and deliverance when we are in trouble but in the end it says: "... and you shall glorify me."

It's often forgotten. In trouble many people cry out or pray to God. HE helps and saves according to HIS word and promise, but then the people often forget the conclusion, saying "Thank you" and praising HIM.

PRAISE does not mean to mumble a small "Thanks" but it has to do with "extol", "make something known", "shout loudly" or "bring it to public".
It excites me, I want to tell others. I want to point to the One who has just solved any problem in a great way. To God, the only true God, the Father of our Lord Jesus Christ. The God of the Bible. That's what the ending of Psalm 50:15 means.

Oh, by the way, did you know this verse in the Bible is also called the emergency number of God?

We all know the emergency number of the police; we are taught that in kindergarten already. If you call the 911 (USA) / 112 or 999 (UK) / 110 (Germany), you will have 100% the police on the other end. At the end of the telephone line, there is someone listening, someone who knows how to help, someone who starts organizing this help for you.

For many years I was working in an operations centre in which we received the emergency calls and where we had to to decide and arrange the first steps of help for the people.
"Emergency call – Police" - I said that thousands of times and then I was listening to where it burns and pinches.
"Mr. Police – I have a problem." And then I arranged adequate help. I know all about it. Don't ask me which kind of action it sometimes was to organize all that.

Mamma mia!

When you "call" (☎ ☺) Psalm 50 : 15, for 100% you will come in touch with the almighty God. That's great, isn't it?

HE also knows about everything
and He becomes active.
In HIS way.
Using HIS possibilities and resources.
In HIS love and wisdom to you.

Which we sometimes don't understand, but in the end it doesn't matter. Sometimes you don´t understand the police either. Actually, it doesn't really matter to you, the main thing is that help comes – that's right?
You trust the Cop on the other side.

The situation was now resolved, but I must confess that I had not been a good example. I had not told my colleague that I would pray. I had not dared. What a shame. What a mighty testimony that would have been for Jesus!
But the way I had done it? Missed up opportunity!
In retrospect, anyone can say anything.

I praised God for His intervention and action – inwardly though – but I had to ask HIM for forgiveness for my cowardliness, for my fear of the opinion of my colleague and for the lost chance to testify HIM.
And HE forgave me – what a relief.

Has it ever happened to you before? Pinched, too shy? Write it down here, ask God for forgiveness and new opportunities. Jesus will give them to you . Then tick off your note and condemnation. Finished! It's done!

Choice of career – "police" or not

A decision for life

I had to deal with the choice of career in the middle of the 70s. That was beside the wife question the 1 million Euro (at that time it was still German Mark) question, this was the "Jackpot-question". We weren't in a position to experiment forever, to try this, to change that, you can change again, you're not in a hurry in life. You have to decide – as quick as possible.

I grew up in a family where I was very well accompanied in my growth and decisions.
My parents and us as children (we are three) were in an evangelical free church.
We loved the fellowship with other people who loved Jesus and HIS Word.

From early on – literally I got it with my mother's milk – I knew that God exists, that HE is the Creator of everything, that His son Jesus died for me so I can go one day to heaven, I knew that His power has no limits.

When I was 13 years old, I made my own clear decision for a life with Jesus. At that time I realized that it is not enough to just know about God or Jesus or to agree with what the Bible says. God wanted my own "OK", voluntarily given. HE wanted to start an adventurous life journey with me but only if I wanted it too. It was my decision.

Yeah - and I wanted exactly that!

So I prayed a very complicated prayer:
"Lord Jesus – I believe in you, you are the Son of God. You died for me, please forgive all my sins, be my Lord. I want to live all my live with you."

It was soooo easy. A clear decision by my own will. Not of my parents or other people. Jesus and me – just two. Like a blood brotherhood. That part with the blood came only from one side, but at least so similar, it was still a blood brotherhood.

And Jesus never let me down, this blood brotherhood still exists since 1970! Wow!

HE has brought me through all the ups and downs of my life, through thick and thin. HE has always been faithful, even in times when I was not that interested in HIM and HIS opinion. HE has always kept me, led me, held me, warned me but sometimes He also let me go because I wanted it and thought I knew it better.
HIS love and my decision for HIM have always surrounded me like a safety fence saving me from the great crash or from getting lost.

And this decision for Jesus was also the basis for my choice of career. I knew, I wanted to become what HE had for me. It wasn't about self-realization, to rake in money, it was about serving God with my profession.

At the end of the process I had two directions, checked and weighed them up against each other, but I couldn´t make a decision. It both seemed to be good, solid, attractive; I could imagine it.

But since a longer period of time I regularly prayed that prayer really seriously:

> "Jesus, please show me
> which job I should choose
> and which woman I should marry.
> Amen!"

And HE showed it to me.
Suddenly I had "the police" on my "scanner", because I picked up a sentence by a school colleague. It wouldn't let me go. My thoughts revolved around the police, I even dreamed about it. (They weren't nightmares, because I had done something wrong in the past. NO!) That was very strange. It was like somebody had switched on a police presentation video in my head. And this video was good. In fact, it was very good. I was more and more warmed up for that job. I discussed it in detail with my parents, asked for their honest assessment and finally we started the application process.
But during this time I also had to face lots of resistance.

It was the time of the late '68s, the rebellion against the establishment, against state order, rebellion against everything that smelled of authority, the Vietnam war and the demonstrations against it, first resistances against nuclear power, flower power, rocker gangs, drugs, hippies, anti-authoritarian education, conscientious objection and similar things.

Society and way of thinking had started to move. A spirit of revolt and rebellion had come over the country.

Also in the Christian "world" many things had started to move. Conscientious objection and alternative military service was so cool and trendy. People looked at you in a really strange way, if you were a Christian and going to the "Bundeswehr" (= German army).
Social jobs were in demand.

Wherever I announced my plans to join the police, I often came into a difficult position. "How can you choose a job where you have to carry a gun?" or "What if you have to shoot?" and similar comments like that. The tenor of all was ultimately: as a Christian, you can´t join the police, you can´t serve the enforcement of state orders, the authorities are the enemy and you have to fight against it. (the Christians! - oh my goodness!)

But something had matured in me. A conviction to do the right thing. And I could feel a great peace, peace and joy in the imagination to work as a policeman and I found more and more arguments for this profession, also or especially as a convinced Christian. I already saw myself as a real Sheriff.

- I am no trigger-happy sheriff who shoots everybody!
- I will give protection and security!
- I am a protecting Cop!
- I can and I must represent Jesus in this job as well, who else will do it?!
- It is a biblical job, established by God! It is written in the Holy Bible!

Huh? Sorry? What? Bible? You are a little bit stupid!
During this time of my personal examination of this difficulty I had always prayed for clarity and confirmation from the Word of God. And God led me to a verse in the Bible. Come on – read with me:

„Everyone must submit to governing authorities.
For all authority comes from God,
and those in positions of authority
have been placed there by God.
So anyone who rebels against authority
is rebelling against what God has instituted,
and they will be punished.
For the authorities do not strike fear in people
who are doing right, but in those who are doing wrong.
Would you like to live without fear of the authorities?
Do what is right, and they will honour you.
The authorities are God's servants, sent for your good.
But if you are doing wrong, of course you should be afraid,
for they have the power to punish you.
They are God's servants,
sent for the very purpose of punishing
those who do what is wrong."
Romans 13 : 1 – 4

„For the Lord's sake,
submit to all human authority
whether the king as head of state,
or the officials he has appointed.
For the king has sent them
to punish those who do wrong
and to honour those who do right.
It is God's will that your honourable lives should silence
those ignorant people
who make foolish accusations against you."
1.Peter 2 : 13 - 15

By this I got a completely new understanding about the government. Why it exists, where it comes from, how it should be. How the Bible sees it.

As a supplement, God showed me another passage from the New Testament, where the soldiers came to John the Baptist and asked how they should act now.

„What should we do?" asked some soldiers.
John replied, "Don't extort money
or make false accusations.
And be content with your pay."
Luke 3 : 14

The Apostle Paul writes here in his letter to the Christians in Rome. They practically lived in the lion's den. The seat of Caesar's government. ...where the power of the state was concentrated and omnipresent.
Where much was done well and much was done badly. Where the abuse of position, corruption, manipulation, patronizing and much more were normal. But where all the good things the Roman state system had were established as well. So obviously all these things had unsettled the Christians in Rome so much that they did not know how to classify it all.

Did Paul say here that we should/must say yes and amen to everything? That everything is right? That we must accept everything? Absolutely not. You can also be against something without immediately rebelling. Having a different opinion and conviction, without reacting with violence, destruction, hatred.

Paul is describing the God-given task of the government and what the behaviour of the people should actually look like.

When we read the Bible, we realize that God is a God of order. Already in the report of the Earth's creation we can see that the Spirit of God was hovering over the "chaos" (the original Hebrew word says: Tohubawohu) before God

34

brought all the pieces – one by one – together in that certain order where they could still be today.

If man had not been on the scene!!!!

We are also told about the Fall of Man, that first Eve and then Adam did what they should not have done. The devil had persuaded them that God was not at all kind to them, that he did not want them to have the best and that he was withholding the best. The devil awakened rebellion, pride and greed in the hearts of the first humans.

A literally diabolic plan.

And the disaster starts ...

...by the "Master of disaster", the Chief of all the Tohubawohu (= chaos), Mr. Dark, the Father of lies, the Organizer of "higgledy-piggledy", the Murderer and Destroyer, the old, ugly Mr. Devil!

(You can read all that in Genesis chapter 1 to 3; Ezekiel 28:11-19; Isaiah 14:1-17 – It's really exciting, gives you a lot of information about the basic things of mankind and it is a real crime thriller of life!)

It is described very clearly how God imagined his world with the people on it. The devil, formerly called Lucifer, was one of the chief angels. Among other things he was responsible for the musical background and sound in heaven, he must have been pretty smart and good and also very beautiful and maybe close to the Mr. Universe. This is how the Bible speaks about in the Scriptures mentioned above.

So this is really hard stuff. Lucifer, one of the highest angels in heaven, had everything you can imagine. He was serving a merciful and loving God. He had a good reputation, God's trust and freedom of action. He was living in that perfect kingdom where everything was richly available. Everything was created for eternal perfection, life, fullness, luck, love and the communion with God. Everything could have been so good.

But then, the unimaginable happened: he became proud because of his God-given position, his beauty and talents and in his heart he developed a rebellious attitude against God. He planned a palace revolution, tempted a bunch of angels and...

... was kicked out with all his followers. "Mr. Brainiac" had seriously thought he could become like God. He, who knew God very well, who had been given trust and love. He, who knew the kingdom of God inside out, who knew all godly principles and how they work. And than he - he starts the revolt. How stupid one must be.

But pride, greed and Wanna-Be had obfuscated his mind. Had eroded his heart. Had brought forth rebellion, hatred, murder and destruction against everything concerning God, His orders, His principles and His people.
Mamma mia!

So that is what we can see day by day when we watch the news on TV, read our little regional newspaper, when our children come home from kindergarten or school and cry while telling us what happened that day. When we experience it ourselves, by being deceived or get into the wrong boat.

That is when we can recognize the handwriting and the working of this Mr. Chaos, that devil, satan, the old snake and his cronies. That is his "business card" for the world. We can recognize him if we want to.

*"**The thief's purpose is to steal and kill and destroy.**
(this is the devil´s handwriting)
My (Jesus) purpose is to give them
a rich and satisfying life.
(Oh – I love Jesus!)
I am the good shepherd.
The good shepherd
sacrifices His life for the sheep."*
John 10 : 10 + 11

Just start watching the news having that scripture in mind. That motive of pride, motive of greed, motive of Wanna-Be, motive of hatred, motive of egoism.
And if you can find these motives single or together, by watching TV, reading the news or whatever, then you also know which handwriting or character this or that has. Then you can estimate if it is from God or from His concurrence.

Oh, by the way: here's a little trick for you now:
If this Mr. Awful, Mr. Dark or Devil, just as you would like to call that enemy of God and the human being, if he once again annoys you, attacks you, wants to tie all kinds of knots on you, does not leave you alone, does not get away from you and reminds you constantly of your past, to make you get into the wrong boat of self-pity – so if he does that, remind him pleasurably about his future!

Take your Bible and read it out loud and with a lot of fun!

For example:
Ezekiel 28 : 11-19
Isaiah 14 : 1-17
Colossians 2 : 14+15
Matthew 25 : 41
Revelations 20 : 10
and much more scriptures …

...
...
...
...
...
...

There are still plenty of verses. Start doing a research about them, pick them out and write them down in here, and you'll have a "punch-back dictionary" soon for you to be reminded. Oh man -I tell you, satan doesn't like these Scriptures. He thinks he is Mr. Stuffed Shirt - but according to the Bible he is nothing! Really nothing! Jesus crushed his head so he got a permanent migraine. Maybe that is why he is so chessed and cranky.

Whatever – it's his own fault!!!

I have no pity for him.

And because these chaotic, destructive and stalling circumstances reigned in the world since the fall of mankind, God came up with something to protect the coexistence of human beings. For the functioning of societies. HE devised plans. Good plans. Very good plans.

A unique, super brilliant Master rescue plan and a Master society plan.

HE has set standards, rules, commandments, which are set so widely, that every human being can move and develop absolutely freely in it, if he respects the limits of the other and does not feel these limits as a threat, because he knows that God is absolutely good and never wants or does anything bad to man.

And HE has brought the master plan to defeat the devil and open up possibilities to stop the actions and plans, to destroy the works of darkness again. HE sent His beloved son Jesus into the race. Jesus walked the path of man here on earth, through all the problems and challenges that this world knows. And HE went this way in complete trust in his Father in heaven, HE did not have to prove himself. The love of God completely enveloped him and so HE could resist all the dirty and slimy attempts to take on the character of the devil or to fall into his trap.

The devil really thought that the master plan was finished when he killed Jesus. So he did. He got people to accuse, condemn and crucify Jesus innocently. He rejoiced as Jesus hung on the cross, his blood dripping slowly to the earth. He saw Jesus with all the sins of the world, the curse of the law and sickness when these deadly things were laid upon Him. But the shot backfired so much! He is still today biting his head off that he did that! (sorry for the slang – but it's true!)

That he no longer realized, out of hatred, the many hints and announcements, prophecies concerning the coming of Jesus, His death and triumphant resurrection and the overwhelming victory over the devil, even though he had known these scriptures by heart for ages and ages.

By His death and resurrection Jesus became a victorious winner, the conqueror of the devil, the restorer of the divine principles on earth, so everyone who entrusts himself to Jesus becomes a child of God in this world, equipped with power, authority and a mission.
That's it - boy!

„In this way, he (Jesus)
disarmed the spiritual rulers and authorities.
(the devil and his fellows)
He shamed them publicly by his victory
over them on the cross."
Colossians 2 : 15

„But to all who believed him (Jesus)
and accepted him,
he gave the right (= authority, power)
to become children of God. "
John 1 : 12

That was a very short excursion why Paul describes this part
with the authorities. Why we need it and how it should work.

Let's put it in a nutshell.
We want to look at it regarding the ideal way, just like God
imagined authorities to be like:

The authority is wanted and appointed by God,
she is a servant of God
for the societies of the world.
Their task is to promote good,
to pursue and punish evil.
The good guy has nothing to fear,
but he who does evil.

ok. that is the ideal, godly standard.

But as I already said … if man had not been!
He is unfortunately prone to perversion, greed, abuse,
selfishness and so on.
We have already learned where all these attitudes come from.

That is why John the Baptist says to the soldiers in the other
passage of the Bible:

Do violence to no one
Do no wrong
Be happy with your pay

It is quite interesting that Jesus did not say here to the soldiers who maintained and enforced the state order at the time of Jesus:
"For heaven's sake, how can you be soldiers! Such a blasphemous profession! You must become pacifists! Get off to the Roman employment office and off to a retraining as a male nurse!"

Noooo! He mentions the three big areas of challenge and danger facing the authorities and their employees:

Abuse of one´s position / authority.
Unlawfulness and inequality before the law
Corruption and greed

And these are still the biggest problems of the authorities in all countries today.
And just because something can go wrong and also does, it does not mean the original concept behind it is bad and useless. On the contrary, the more people behave correctly, the less goes wrong - on both sides.

And so my journey began as a newly graduated Cop in February 1976, a decision that had matured, prayed through, been confirmed by God and, thanks to the loving support of my parents, was put into practice.
I was with the Bavarian Police Troops!

I knew I was right. I belong to the "Servants of God", an instrument of the almighty God.

Here is some space for you to write down things you read in the newspaper, that you realized in relation to the diabolical motives we recently talked about. And then you'll realize how our society has been affected. (I'm afraid there's not enough space.)

Let me give you a first example:

Diesel fumes scandal   Motive: unscrupulous greed
(Volkswagen, Audi...)

…......................................   …..

Overlooked excavation...

... or how to get a Volkswagen Van back on the road again

One evening I drove alone in the patrol car, it was a Volkswagen Van (VW Bus), to a family in the city to conduct an interrogation. It was already dark, it was late. The man I wanted to interrogate hadn't come home from work earlier.

When I arrived and parked by the house, I noticed a construction pit that was not really well secured. I still thought that I would have to ask the man about it, or rather arrange for proper protection.
So I conducted the interrogation, time was going by, we were still talking about a lot of stuff, and - I forgot about the excavation.

When I wanted to drive back to the station, I went this time from the other side to the VW bus, without passing the pit, got in and drove backwards. I turned the wheels and after a short distance backwards - there was a heavy bang.

I was fossilized, sitting in my bus and slowly it dawned on me what had happened. I had driven into the pit with my right rear wheel and was now sitting up with the vehicle chassis.
Oh my goodness.
I got out of the car and realized that nothing was damaged or broken. I just sat up.

Now good advice was "quite expensive" and I thought about the possibilities. I always came to the same result with all alternatives: call a tow truck, get the colleagues, etc:

"They're laughing their heads off!
And I'm the laughingstock!
Embarrassed to the bone,
the mockery of the entire department."

The whole scene of jokes, gags, allusions and mockery that the police assortment had to offer among colleagues ran before my inner eye. True to the slogan: If you have colleagues, you don't need enemies!

And again I had only the prayer that God should get me out of this misery, out of this embarrassing situation, no matter how.

And that is what I find so brilliant about HIM. Since I had consciously decided for Him, the Word of God had taken on a whole new dimension. It was HIS word for MY life and MY circumstances. No magic word register in the Harry Potter style according to the motto: "for VW buses in construction pits you have to speak magic formula 54345cv45-hocus-pocus-fidibus" and then he is out again.

Not like this.

The Word of God has answers to all questions and challenges of life. They are written in the Bible and can and want to be discovered with the Spirit of God, HIS Holy Spirit, believed and to be used in trust and under HIS instruction. And for this he often uses reports from other people who have already experienced the almost impossible with Jesus, who have had their own trust in God and courage to dare to do the impossible.

And that's what "faith" means. I trust in HIS word, in HIS love for me and HIS care for me, in HIS resources and unimaginable possibilities.

And that came back to me!

Jesus walked on water and so did Peter! (Sure, I wasn't Jesus or Peter, but Peter was able to - at least for a while)

Jesus fed over 5000 people with only a few fish sandwiches. (The food multiplied again and again the more HE distributed - blatant! I like fish burgers!)

Moses divided the Red Sea, because there was no ferry for a few 100.000 people.

Samson had power without end and carried whole city gates up to the mountain.
(Rambo is a wishy – washy Tarzan against it)

And then there are moments when God gives you a special word for the moment to handle a situation. And this word releases through the Holy Spirit, connected with my faith, trust and courage, a power that you cannot imagine.

„The LORD is my light and my salvation
so why should I be afraid?
The LORD is my fortress, protecting me from danger,
so why should I tremble?"
Psalm 27 : 1

„For I can do everything through CHRIST,
who gives me strength!"
Philippians 4 : 13

And that is exactly what happened in that moment. These bible scriptures which came into my mind set their power free in my heart and faith. My mind was fighting with hands and feet (or something like that) against what was about to happen. Faith in action!

I put it in neutral, released the brake. Nothing more could happen, the VW bus was stuck in the hole. Then I went to the rear right wheel arch, where the bus was sat on, grabbed the wheel arch (they were still very solid in this time) with both hands and lifted the VW bus out. I pushed it right over the hole, let go, got in, steered the front wheel around the pit and drove to the department.

Whistling indifferently I came back and did my paperwork as if nothing had happened.

I didn't tell them. They wouldn't have believed me anyway. And I didn't feel like having funny discussions.

Outwardly, I was Mr. Cool - but inside, I was all agitated, excited and confused at the same time, full of adrenaline; I could hardly believe it myself. Even today, when I think about it, I get goose bumps about the power of God and His Word. And now it was just a ragged VW bus, good old thick metal, engine in the back, how many kilos at the rear? 1000? I don't know - okay?
What happens when God does something really heavy?

You can call me "Münchhausen" (a figure in a German fairy tale who always experienced unbelievable stories) or any other storyteller. But it's true. That's what I stand for. Why should I lie to you? I haven't got any profit.

I experienced this a few times in my life, but I'm not telling you these stories here, otherwise I have nothing left for my next book. I'm sorry. ☺ ☺ ☺

Another world...

... U 903 on a combat patrol
(U 903 - designation and number for a German submarine WWII)

It is a very exciting situation when you have to deal with people who are somehow completely out of it. But harmless. And there are many of them. They don't attract attention, they are harmless, as I said, they only get in the way of certain people.

According to my observations over the last 40 years, usually during a full moon. This phenomenon is often described, but it is scientifically denied that there is any connection. Well, they should, that's not the point.

Ask nurses, paramedics, policemen, people who work at the front line, right next to them, who deal with such people. They'll tell you a lot about full moon and abnormalities in people.

One episode always happened only on full moon nights. For years. We knew him, liked him, waited for him in the marketplace ... and then he came along!

Full moon - the streets deserted - nobody far and wide - lonely at the roadside a patrol car - two Cops waiting for the monthly recurring spectacle:

U 903 on a combat patrol!

A Ford Sierra, light blue. We all knew this vehicle, knew the older man who drove it, alone in the vehicle, well-groomed appearance.

He sees the patrol car, brakes, stops on the right and jumps out.
Standing next to his car, he takes up a soldier's posture, puts his right hand on his non-existent cap and makes a report in the barracks sound:

> "Report obediently,
> U 903 on a combat patrol,
> no enemy ships sighted!"

When I first dealt with him, I could hardly believe that something like this existed. My bear trainer had warned me. And then you stand in front of him - skeptical and cautious. Is he dangerous? Does he attack you? What's next?

In the beginning I tried to talk to him normally, tried to convince him with reasonable arguments that the war was over long time ago; that this is not the Atlantic Ocean, but the market place of a small town, and that he doesn't have a submarine, but a Ford Sierra.

I realized quite quickly that my arguments did not get through to him. My colleague let me do it with a smile.

Patrol Luke 12 / 3" against „U-903".

A vintage police VW Beetle against a steel colossus from a German war dockyard.

I could not reach him in those moments. He did not respond to normal speech. He was good-natured, not aggressive in any way, not dangerous, not rebellious, ... he was simply on his combat patrol. This was his world under a full moon.

The interesting thing was that if you met him outside the full moon and talked to him, he was completely normal. He didn't know about U 903. He was like a sleepwalker.
He also drove his car safely, obeyed traffic regulations, etc. There was no reason for us to take him out of circulation.
Apparently the full moon created a flashback in his mind.

Here a small interesting definition from *WIKIPEDIA:*
A "FLASHBACK" (English expression, literally: fulgurous back, free translated as: re-experience or reverberation memory) is a psychological phenomenon, which is caused by a key stimulus. The affected person then has a sudden, usually powerful re-experience of a past experience or previous emotional states. These memories can be of any imaginable type of feeling.
The term is mainly used when the memory appears involuntarily and/or when it is so strong that the person relives the experience, unable to recognize it completely as a memory.
Status: 01.01.2018)

… which brought him back to his days in the „Wehrmacht".

And I had met many people like him. There were also guys who then became aggressive and vicious, with whom we had to fight, but I'd rather not talk about that here.

What do you do with a buddy like that now? The normal doesn't work. The only thing I could think of at that moment was that I had to meet him somehow in his "world" in order to be able to talk to him. And to get him to do what I actually wanted him to do, namely to go home and get into bed.

Well then - to put to the touch:

I built myself up in front of him, (he obviously saw me as a higher officer, otherwise he would not have reported to me.) Right hand to the greeting and message response to my non-existent naval cap and told him in the commanding military tone:

„Seaman Meier!
(so he was called, the rank was guessed)
Thanks for the report, he should step down!
(in the third person, ancient speech,
also used in rural areas in Germany for a long time until the 90`s)
and immediately return to your home port.
Finish the combat patrol and let him rest."

He greeted promptly, repeated the order in short form as prescribed: "Yes, I understood! "finish combat patrol, home port, rest, roger!"
jumped into his U 903 - uh - his Ford Sierra and drove away.

We followed him at a distance, he actually drove home, drove into the garage. He went into the house, we saw the light for a moment, then silence in the ship - uh - house. The night was quiet.

The game and the speeches were repeated every month at full moon. Science or no science.
I don't know how long he was out at night on his combat patrol when we couldn't stop him because of other missions. Probably all night or until his petrol ran out. He wasn't torpedoed - of course not.

Another example where I developed even more acting talent was...

The Naked Nun ...
... an old lady finds peace

We had a very old widow in the city who lived alone in her little house. She was well known in the office because she also had a "push", as we called it. She had no relatives, nobody was known who could take care of her. She had a kind of persecution complex, but harmless, almost cute. To me. For her, it was a real emotional life pain.

One day it was my turn (it was perhaps 30 - 35 years ago now) to go to her place, she had called again because she was being spied on. (??? Hey – what's going on???)

Ok, that's always the balancing act in such operations, you know that the facts are not really true, but you can never be sure that this time there might not be something more to it. Besides, these people develop a strong persistence and keep calling until a patrol actually comes.

So we come to the little house and ring the bell. The Granny opens the door, dressed up pico-bello and also with her hair, no signs of neglect or disorder. Also in the house everything in its place and clean.

So I introduce myself. "Good afternoon, "Wachtmeister" (means: constable) Kunstmann from the department XY. You called us. What is the problem and how can we help you?"
(I have often referred to myself as a "Constable" = „Wachtmeister" to older people, regardless of my actual rank. Most people have no idea with the rank. But "Wachtmeister" was a well-known term).

She tells me with full conviction that a crazy artist has moved in above her, who has drilled a hole through the ceiling in her bedroom and now watches her undressing and going to bed every evening. He also painted a naked nun on the outside of her door.

Upon my soul, what a sex gangster!

I look at Grandma, she looks at me. She was completely serious and worried. I was about to burst out laughing - inside, of course. I wasn't allowed to show that I didn't take her seriously.
That was quite a story! The naked nun (how can you recognize her?) and a Peep Show in the evening.
Ok - all right.

Then I asked her, quite innocently and in an official manner, how one could recognize that it was a nun - if she was naked?

Totally uncomprehendingly the old lady looked at me and then just said: "Well - at the coif!"
Of course. What else could I have been thinking about? I should have known. I nodded understandingly and successfully fought the bursting laughter cramp.

What do you do in a situation like that?
I had learned that you had to take these people, who for all kinds of reasons perceive things differently, seriously in order to meet them in their own world and help them as much as possible.

Today this is often different, confused people are immediately reported to the regulatory authority or brought there, in acute cases they are admitted to a mental hospital. In the past, such things were handled to the best of our knowledge and ability. Psychiatric clinic was a foreign word, for all the paperwork you had to find a colleague who knew which forms to fill out.

Today, almost no shift passes in which people of different ages have to be brought to the psychiatric clinic.

So I explained to the old lady that this was a case of particularly serious impertinence and that we would put a stop to the painter now and forever.
The lady looked at me surprised, probably I was the first in a long line of colleagues who had already been involved with her who took her seriously.

So I went with her into the house and she showed me the "Peep-Show-Hole" in the bedroom. She pointed to a small dark spot on the white ceiling.

"That's what he drilled into it, and he always looks through it, the lecher!"
She was completely outraged.
On the ceiling was actually - nothing! Only a small dark mark.

And now I slowly came into my element. From childhood I had a vivid fantasy, acting talent and enough boldness to do crazy things.

To the horror of my colleague I told her: "You are very lucky that we are here today. ...because we're specialists in these things and we have special equipment."

I looked at my colleague and saw that he was wondering which of the two, the Cop or Grandma, would have to go to the nuthouse.

I let the Granny show me the picture of the Naked Nun, she pointed to the outside of her kitchen door. There was absolutely nothing there.

I hesitated for a moment, but she said that you could only see it from a certain angle. She had already tried several times to wash it away, but it would not work.

I was a dunderhead! - of course - the special angle. I could have figured it out for myself. And so I agreed with her and confirmed that this really was a blasphemous picture and that we would have to get it removed in any case.

I also explained to her in all seriousness that I would mix a special liquid and wash the picture off. This liquid would also seal the door in such a way that nobody would ever be able to paint anything on it again.

I asked her to go to my colleague and stay with him, because nobody was allowed to watch the mixing of the liquid, after all it was a secret police tincture.

She went to my completely shocked colleague and waited there eagerly. So I went to the kitchen, where I suspected detergent under the sink. And right. Everything that belongs in a proper household was there. I took an old enamel bowl and started pouring some harmless cleaning products together. Preferably under loud clatter.

Then, in front of the woman's eyes and the wide open eyes and mouth of my colleague, I washed the kitchen door outside wet.
Afterwards I asked Grandma to come in for an inspection, because I had seen that her face had brightened up and she began to radiate.

I asked her if she would see anything else. "Please have a good look at the door from all angles".
And she did it thoroughly and then she fell around my neck.
"All gone! This mess is gone! No more Naked Nun! Thank you very much, what would I have done without you, I'm so

lucky that you were on patrol today, the specialists!"

She was so happy and unburdened. I had gotten through to her world with a little theatre and had solved her problem.
In a similar way I also closed the "Peep-Show-Hole" in her bedroom ceiling and assured her that this layer that I had sprayed over it could no longer be pierced.

She wanted to give us money, she was so thankful.
We said goodbye with the comment that we would not take the money under any circumstances, after all that is what the police are there for, to help people obtain their rights and protect them from indecent painters.

We drove away and we never had a call again from the old lady . Really - never again - for years - the whole department!

My colleague asked me how I came up with such a crazy idea. I could only tell him that it had come to me spontaneously, because I wanted to help the Granny somehow.

Now someone could say that I had lied and deceived the poor woman completely and that it was not right.

I can only say that I did not see it as a lie then and I do not see it as a lie now, at the end of my time in the police.

For me it was and is an unusual, but necessary measure to help this woman and also other people who no longer live in our world. She was confused due to her age, but only in a small area of her thinking. I didn't want to do her any harm, I didn't want to give myself an advantage, I didn't want to talk myself out of it, nothing of the sort. Just help her. Just to get through to her world.

In my opinion their conspicuousness and behavior had an organic cause, as with so many old people I have dealt with.

Which reminds me, this is a little bit like in the Bible.
Man had distanced himself so far from God, his Creator and provider, that he no longer perceived Him, no longer heard Him. He was only fighting for survival in his small, miserable world, fighting his neighbour, drowning in his sin and its consequences and being lost forever. (Do you remember what I said earlier about the Mr. Chaos, that Mr. Dark?)

And that is why God sent his son.
From the heavenly kingdom into the natural world.
From the perfection of God into the imperfection of man.
From a perfect environment into an imperfect one.
From eternity into a temporal, transient world.
From God´s Kingdom of Peace into a world of injustice, murder and strife.
Jesus dived into the confused, fallen world to create a way out of it.
HE dived into a lost, dying world to pave a way for salvation and redemption.
HE, the Son of God, became the Son of Man so that we could hear, understand and know God again.

So that the fundamental problem of man could be solved for everyone who trusts in Jesus.

HE, Jesus, met us in our confused world to make a clear announcement.

„Jesus told him,
I am the way, the truth, and the life.
No one can come to the Father except through me. "
John 14 : 6

„However, those the Father has given me will come to me,
and I will never reject them."
John 6 : 37

GOD made himself understandable again, in our language, with our means, focused on our perception.
And HE was very good at it.
HE made it!

„For this is how God loved the world:
He gave his one and only Son,
so that everyone who believes in him
will not perish but have eternal life.
God sent his Son into the world
not to judge the world,
but to save the world through him."
John 3 : 16 + 17

„You must have the same attitude that Christ Jesus had.
Though he was God,
he did not think of equality with God
as something to cling to.
Instead, he gave up his divine privileges;
he took the humble position of a slave
and was born as a human being.
When he appeared in human form,
he humbled himself in obedience to God
and died a criminal's death on a cross.
Therefore, God elevated him
to the place of highest honour
and gave him the name above all other names,
that at the name of Jesus every knee should bow,
in heaven and on earth and under the earth,
and every tongue declare that Jesus Christ is Lord,
to the glory of God the Father!"
Philippians 2 : 5 – 11

„Since he (Jesus) himself
has gone through suffering and testing,
he is able to help us when we are being tested. "
Hebrews 2 : 18

Wow - what a description of "Mission Earth" of Jesus.
The "Mission -Become Human- so we can understand Him again"!!!

How pitiful were my efforts to be heard in the world of the "U-903" and the "Naked Nun"! But I have tried anyway, on my own level, with my possibilities, with human success and yet there is nothing to compare with how perfectly Jesus has done it.

With the phenomenon of "confusion" there are often organic causes but also spiritual causes as well which can confuse a person. And here, special tincture and a credibly played show is not enough.

Confused "traffic policeman"...

... and how the love of God comes into the bullpen

Before the next experience I have to say that in those days, and it is now more than 20 years ago, I did not yet have the understanding and revelation about spiritual authority, demons and liberation in Christ that I have today. Today the story would probably end differently.

I was inside the office when we received a call that a confused young man was standing on a busy intersection and was directing traffic. I sent a patrol to check it out and take the young man into custody. They should take him to the police station.

The patrol brought him in after a while. They didn't know what to do. They couldn't get anything out of him. Every question about him or something else he laughed out loud and sneered. He twisted his eyes until you could only see the white and twisted and twisted his arms, hands and fingers in a completely unnatural way. He articulated himself only like an animal, with screeching and grunting, it was like in a horror movie.

For his own safety and because we couldn't just leave him in the station with the other public traffic, we locked him up in a cell for our and his protection. He was not injured, he had nothing with which he could get hurt. The patrol had already checked him thoroughly and they hoped to find something that would point to his person, but unfortunately nothing like that.

While he waited in the bullpen in the basement, we tried to find out who he might be and whether he was missing or escaped somewhere.

We phoned the hospitals and homes, we checked the current manhunts - without success.

Finally I decided to go to him and handle the case with my faith and with the name of Jesus. Let's see what that would do. I was not yet so firm in this combination.

I took a young police trainee with me so that I would not be alone with the confused guy.
I instructed the young colleague to stand at the door and if necessary calling for help and be a witness to whatever happened.
He was a little bit worried, but he went with me because he had to go, claro! I was the boss.

In the corridor in front of the cells there was nothing else to be heard. We approached his cell quietly and I looked through the spyhole. It could be that he was pretending something. But he sat quietly on his bunk.

I unlocked the outer door, at that moment he jumped up, twisted everything again and roared and bellowed like an animal.
Our backs gave us goose bumps and the hairs on the back of our necks stood up (I had a little more hair at that time).

But I was determined and I knew that in this case I only could go ahead with the name of Jesus. I mean, I didn't know much about this area of demonic things back then, it was practically new territory for me, but as the saying goes: " What you have to do - do it !"

At that moment I felt such a boldness like never before.

An inner voice seemed to tell me: "Don't be afraid, I'm with you!" I recognized Jesus in that voice.

I approached the second cell door. Behind this door the young man was roaring and shouting.

I ordered him in a loud, firm voice:
"Look at me!"

And behold, he stopped, looked at me, roared and grunted still loudly. He still twisted his arms and hands, but he looked at me.

I thought to myself: OK, that seems to work, keep watching. And I went on.

"Be quiet, stop raving, in the name of Jesus!"

Bam! It was like they cut off his electricity. In one second he was silent, stood still, his arms hung down completely straight and powerless, he looked at me spellbound.

"I'm coming in to you now.
Sit down on the bunk and keep quiet."

He sat down and kept quiet.

Before I closed up, I made sure that the young colleague was on guard. I asked him: "Mike, how are you? Everything ok?"

He stood chalk-white at the door and whispered, "You're not going in there, he's dangerous!"

But I knew in that moment that he wouldn't hurt me. The faith in Jesus and his word made me safe and strong.

Mike had realized that this now was something religious and had folded his hands well and automatically, as if he was in prayer. Probably he had just managed to avoid the "sign of the cross", but that is now only a guess.

So I unlocked the door and took the first step into the cell. Suddenly the confused guy spoke to me in a dark but clearly understandable voice. A voice out of the fridge, a voice out of a grave, a voice out of a nightmare.

"Leave me alone or I'll kill you."

At that moment I knew exactly what was going on and who was speaking.

Suddenly Bible scriptures came to my mind that described similar situations and fitted exactly to my situation:

,, So they (Jesus and his disciples) *arrived at the other side of the lake, in the region of the Gerasenes.*

When Jesus climbed out of the boat,
a man possessed by an evil spirit
came out from a cemetery to meet him.

This man lived among the burial caves
and could no longer be restrained, even with a chain.

Whenever he was put into chains and shackles
-as he often was-
he snapped the chains from his wrists
and smashed the shackles.
No one was strong enough to subdue him.

Day and night he wandered among the burial caves
and in the hills, howling and cutting himself
with sharp stones.

When Jesus was still some distance away,
the man saw him, ran to meet him,
and bowed low before him.

With a shriek, he screamed:
"Why are you interfering with me,
Jesus, Son of the Most High God?
In the name of God, I beg you, don't torture me!"

For Jesus had already said to the spirit,
"Come out of the man, you evil spirit."
Then Jesus demanded, "What is your name?"
And he replied, "My name is Legion,
because there are many of us inside this man."
Mark 5 : 1 – 9

„Suddenly, a man in the synagogue
who was possessed by an evil spirit began shouting,
"Why are you interfering with us,
Jesus of Nazareth?
Have you come to destroy us?
I know who you are : The Holy One of God!"
Jesus cut him short.
"Be quiet! Come out of the man," he ordered.
At that, the evil spirit screamed,
threw the man into a convulsion,
and then came out of him."
Mark 1 : 23 – 26

„For we are not fighting
against flesh-and-blood enemies,
but against evil rulers and authorities of the unseen world,
against mighty powers in this dark world,
and against evil spirits in the heavenly places. "
Ephesians 6 : 12

„ When the seventy-two disciples returned,
they joyfully reported to him,
"Lord, even the demons obey us
when we use your name!"

"Yes," he (Jesus) told them,
"I saw Satan fall from heaven like lightning!

Look, I have given you authority
over all the power of the enemy,
and you can walk among snakes
and scorpions and crush them.
Nothing will injure you.

But don't rejoice because evil spirits obey you;
rejoice because your names are registered in heaven."
Luke 10 : 17 - 20

The Bible speaks very clearly about evil spirits and demons that torment people and make their lives difficult. Not everyone is totally possessed in the same way, but evil forces can come into life and influence, torment, disturb and make life difficult.

There are many doors that people can open for such demons and forces, consciously or unconsciously.

Such doors can be and very often are:

Drug use (any kind of drugs – even "light" - like dope)
Read horoscopes (even if you don't believe in them)
Lay cards (Tarot, ...)
Astrology (your future is in the stars, ...)
Black or White Magic
Spiritualism
Satanism in any form

64

Blood contracts to Satan, spirits or humans
Secret societies, gang memberships
and much more....

Even Homeopathy is not harmless and without a purpose! (is without active and natural substances, but not without effect on the user. It opens his mind to supernatural, unknown forces and powers, to witchcraft).

The " creator " of Homeopathy, Samuel Hahnemann
(*10. April 1755 in Meißen / Germany; † 2. Juli 1843 in Paris / France)
had said that it was not about what was in it, but about discovering the spirit behind the substance. Hahnemann himself called it **witchcraft**.

Indication of source:
"Organon der rationellen Heilkunde", published 1810, § 269, 6th edition, after the edition of Richard Haehl 1921

"Homeopathic medicine develops the inner, spiritual medicinal powers of the raw substances to a previously unheard of degree by means of a peculiar treatment, which was unattempted until my time, whereby they all become very, indeed immeasurably, penetratingly effective and helpful (Haehl)

Original text Hahnemann: Long before this invention of mine, several changes had already become known through experience, which are brought about in various natural substances by rubbing; e.g. warmness, heat, fire, development of odours in bodies that are odourless in and of themselves, magnetisation of steel, etc.
However, all these properties produced by rubbing were only related to the physical and lifeless; But the law of nature, according to which physiological and pathogenic forces, which change the condition of the living organism, are produced by rubbing and shaking in the raw material of medicines, and even in natural substances which have never been proven to be medicinal, on condition that this is done by means of the interposition of a non medical (indifferent) medium in certain conditions - This wonderful physical, but exquisitely physiological-pathogenic law of nature had not been discovered before my time. What a miracle, then, if the present heralds of nature and physicians (herewith still unknown) up to now have thought of the magical healing power of the, according to homeopathic teaching prepared (dynamisirten) and in such a small gift
applied drugs, not believed so far"

Okay, here was obviously some kind of spirit at work. Because if there had been a normal psychological or organic cause, the young man's behaviour would not have changed because of my announcement. You could see that with the other colleagues. Nothing else had happened.

But here? Here was something different. Here collided two spiritual dimensions . I didn't know much then; not what I know today. But the confrontation was suddenly there, just because I had entered the bullpen and was not impressed by the circus the spirit did. Not even the death threat. I knew who I was and who was on my side and who was the one who spoke through the poor young guy.

And the spirit was under my orders!
I wasn't intimidated, but looked at the young man firmly (in fact, I looked right through him to the spirit behind the whole action) and said like to a third person in the room:

"You will shut up now in Jesus' name,
I'm going to speak with the young man now!"

Immediately the whole behaviour of the man changed, he was calm, looked at me with clear eyes and waited for me. I sat down next to him on the bunk (the colleague was still standing at the door with folded hands and probably thought he was in a science fiction movie, he couldn't believe what he saw).

I saw in the young man only a tortured person and I asked him what was wrong with him and how he had come to this condition.

And the unbelievable happened.
He started to talk in a normal voice, just like two friends are talking.

He was very good in school, but not good enough for his parents. They kept pushing him to do better. He tried his best, but that was all that was possible for him. The parents kept pushing him, became aggressive, beat him to force him to read the books and make him better. It was a martyrdom.

One day, when the pressure was once again super great, it made "click" in his head and he was in that condition. Like someone else is controlling his head now. That had been many years ago now.

I asked him if he was placed in a home.
He denied that, he lived at home with the parents. Normally he takes strong pills, then these confusions or strange effects would be almost completely gone. Today he had not taken his pills and had escaped from home.

I asked him for his personal details, the names of his parents and his telephone number.

Without hesitation he told me what I wanted and I wrote it down.

Then I started to tell him about the love of God and that Jesus died for him on the cross. That his situation did not come from God and that Jesus loved him infinitely. The young man literally sucked this message from my lips and he cried softly. I felt that Jesus was now here with him in the cell and embraced him. That he could now invite Jesus to come into his life and take care of him. That he could accept Jesus as Lord and Saviour, so that one day he could spend eternity in heaven with Jesus together.

When I asked him if he wanted to receive Jesus into his life, he said without hesitation and with a smile on his face "YES - I want that!" and we prayed together. Together we prayed the prayer of salvation. He prayed with me, affirmed it with all his heart, he gave his life into the hand of Jesus Christ and I felt the peace of God coming into his heart.

He was over the moon. So I am too!

I now explained the further procedure to him. I would inform his mother, she would come to pick him up, he should be patient a little longer, nothing more would happen to him.

I embraced him like a son and said goodbye for the moment. I left the cell, locked it and when I turned around again he was in his confused condition again. I had never experienced anything like this before. It was as if a time window had closed again.

I went upstairs with my Mike, who was deathly pale and could not understand what he had just experienced. I explained it to him as best I could.

Up in the office the colleague asked me what we had done for so a long time, as there was nothing to get out of this guy anyway.

I answered him: "Well we talked, what else could we have done?
"Yes - yes, talk, of course!" he replied mockingly.

Then he looked at my young Mike, who at first nodded his head wordlessly and violently and came out: "That's all true - he talked to him - he got it all out of him."

Wordlessly I went to the phone and called the mother and explained to her where her son was and that she would please pick him up.

Now even the mocking colleague was pale and speechless.

Some time later the mother came, we fetched her junior from the cell and handed him over to her care.

His behaviour was much calmer, no more dislocations or strange noises. But he was in another world again. He was no longer responsive.

When they went out the door, I still spoke to him again directly and loudly. "And remember who loves you!"
He turned around, shining all over his face and said in a crystal clear voice: "Jesus - I will never forget that! Thank you."

… he spoke and went home with his mother.

At this point I would like to emphasize again that it was one of my first experiences of this kind. The knowledge and understanding of spiritual authority develops, not everything is immediately there, I had grown in these areas over the time and learned more of these things. And that is what practical opportunities are for, besides the theory.

Today I would command that spirit to disappear, to let go the young man. And the ghost would have to let him go. Because it would be in the name of Jesus. The name which is given all power and authority in heaven and on earth. The name to which every knee must bow, every defeated demon and devil (and they are - defeated forever) must obey. Because of the name of JESUS!

I often experienced this in the last years, manifestations of demonic powers in the life and bodies of people. And they had to go because I commanded them in the name of Jesus.

Oh yes - since that episode I was the man for "special cases" in the department.

Before we continue, a short example.

Here you can write down if you ever had strange encounters and how you would react and act today, after you know and will hear more through this book.

Bound in chains...

... police and church

A few years ago we visited some churches in Argentina. One evening we were invited for dinner in a church.

When we arrived, the pastor told us that we did not have that long, at 10 pm the police would bring a possessed guy. No mental clinic would accept him anymore because he was so aggressive and totally crazy. We thought that was a certain exaggeration.

Shortly before 10 p.m. a few more strong men (members of this church) came into the church, along with church elders and they went into a room at the back.

Few minutes afterwards there was a knock on the door, outside was the police! They brought a 40 year old man, completely wild and tied up with thick chains. I had never seen anything like this. He behaved wildly, roared in an inhuman voice, but was handed over to the men from the church. The policemen were glad to get rid of him and drove away quickly.

We finished our visit and left the pastor with his men and the possessed.

Two days later we heard that they had delivered the man from these demons in the name of Jesus and that he was now completely normal. The local police would bring people like this man more often to the church because they would help them in a way that no clinic could do. For the police only the result counts, not the name of the church or denomination.

It was amazing.

In the past years my wife and I have learned a lot in this subject of deliverance and we have been able to help many people with demonic bonds in the name of Jesus and set them free. This has nothing to do with classical or church exorcism. I do not understand anything about this. I am not interested either. We only pray for the people and command the demons out of the person in the name of Jesus.

At this point I'd like to say that I wrote my first book a few years ago. It's called "Acts 29" and it was published by the same publisher as this one. (BOD-Verlag/Norderstedt)

In this book I describe some things in connection with deliverance in the name of Jesus and how I see things from the Bible. Also many healings and personal experiences by faith. But more I will not reveal here.

Read more about it at the end of this book.

Where will you spend eternity? ...

... There is no way around JESUS CHRIST

As mentioned in previous chapter, in this chapter I will talk about something existential. Something that is important to me and you should know about.

It is about YOUR life. Yes exactly - you read correctly - it is about YOU.

Not primarily about your physical life, but about your spiritual life.

I don't know if you have ever thought about it, but you should definitely do so. Because that is the all-important question: Where will you spend eternity?

With Jesus together in His Kingdom for all eternity or separated from God and Jesus in eternal damnation?

I want to tell you about an experience:

We were on patrol and were told to drive to a serious accident. A motorcyclist had been run over.
Well, these are not exactly the nicest jobs during the patrol, but they are part of it and unfortunately they are the order of the day.

The young man was miraculously, thank God, not so badly injured and was taken to hospital. He was responsive.

We first took care of the accident on site, had the damaged vehicles towed away and then drove to the hospital to talk to the motorcyclist and write down his accident data.

He was in a reasonably good mood and after completing the formalities we started talking about the accident. I explained to him on the basis of the overall circumstances, the traces and accident investigations that he had had a great guardian angel. He should be glad that he is still alive.

And so we came to the question mentioned at the beginning, where he would now spend eternity if the guardian angel had not been here?

He became a bit insecure and tried to put the topic down a bit and he tried to be "cool". But I didn't let him go and asked again and again if he knew God and what his attitude was to Him. If he really knew where he would be when he died.

He then honestly told me that he already believed in "God up there somehow", that he had been baptised as a baby and that he hoped that this would be enough for heaven. After all, the priest had told him so and promised him.

He lay in front of me in the hospital bed, his leg tied up thickly and I felt so sorry for him. The guy had no idea about eternity, had no real relationship with God and Jesus but still hoped that it would be enough?

Mamma mia! Had no one really told him?

That baby baptism has nothing to do with "coming to heaven", → really nothing at all?
It is just to make the baby a little bit wet and make it crying. The baby understands nothing.

This „promise" of the priest is one of the biggest lies on earth. I´m sorry – I don´t know how they come on this idea. The Bible speaks nothing, nothing about „Baby Baptism"!!!!!!!!

But back to the guy in the hospital.
Doesn't he know that...

... that only a relationship with Jesus is the ticket to HIM?
…that you can't get past Jesus?
…that Jesus loved him infinitely and died for him?
…that Jesus is waiting for a response, an invitation?
…that it only works if you bring Jesus into your life and ask for forgiveness?
... that you can and should live with Jesus?

I thought about how I could explain it to him in the best way and prayed silently for an idea.
And it came!

I had a freshly injured man here, who had been taken care of by the ambulance and hospitalized. He had great luck (?) (!)

And so I explained it to him in my own way.
"You know, when you had the accident and you were lying there, did it help that you knew there was an ambulance? No. Knowing that, even if it's 1000% true, won't help you. You'll bleed to death.

Yes, there's a paramedic (EMP), one that's highly trained. who is ready to go day and night. Who will do everything possible to help you. Who will risk his own life to save yours. It's not enough to know that there's an ambulance or paramedic. It won't just come on its own, it has to be called.
He also knows that accidents happen, but he only comes when he is needed and wanted.

Have you ever noticed that emergency doctors don't patrol the streets, like the motto: "Let's see if we see a seriously injured person lying around somewhere, who we can put a band-aid on" or "Well - then we'll just injure one ourselves, so that we can doctor him and look good.

Hey buddy, there's nothing like this!

Jesus is waiting for an invitation from YOU. HE stands ready to save YOU, to liberate YOU, to restore YOU. But HE is waiting for YOUR own, voluntary decision! Do YOU want to invite Jesus? Do YOU want to entrust and hand over YOUR life to Him? Will YOU trust Him?"

The guy had understood this example and this question. This was a perfect match for his situation. I told him what the Bible says.

(We already had this today, with this emergency number of God, remember?:)

> *„Then call on me when you are in trouble,*
> *and I will rescue you,*
> *and you will give me glory."*
> Psalm 50 : 15
> (Hey – GOD is waiting for your call ☎)

Other biblical scriptures illustrate it as follows:

> *„Listen!*
> *The LORD 's arm is not too weak to save you,*
> *nor is his ear too deaf to hear you call. "*
> Isaiah 59 : 1

> *„For the Son of Man (Jesus) came*
> *to seek and save those who are lost. "*
> Luke 19 : 10

„But to all who believed Him (Jesus)
and accepted Him,
(into their lives, under HIS management)
He gave the right to become children of God. "
John 1 : 12

And so we prayed together directly in the hospital room. A young man was saved, he gave his life to Jesus, who became his Saviour and Lord from that moment on.

I gave him the address of a good church in his neighborhood and promised to call him again.

A few weeks later, he was completely recovered, I called him and asked him how he was doing. He replied that he was now going to this church I mentioned and was learning and experiencing more about Jesus and faith. He was doing super well.

At this point I also ask YOU, do YOU know where YOU will spend YOUR eternity?

You have read up to here and you might think to yourself: This is not possible! I've never seen or heard anything like this. I only know God or Jesus from religious education in school which was boring. My grandmother told me something about it, but it was not really exciting. I had to go to church as a child, it was totally boring. This Jesus and all that faith stuff is strange to life, wrong and quite a hypocrisy.

You may be partly right, because you may have had profound negative experiences in the past.

If you have been disappointed in the past by people using the name of God or the name of Jesus, who were supposed to tell you about love and salvation, but instead abused you mentally, physically or spiritually, those who did not tell you the truth from the Bible, made false promises (baby baptism and heaven, etc.!) and ultimately robbed your interest in Jesus, the good kingdom of God and an overflowing life in Jesus Christ. I am totally sorry for you. I really am.

But God is not to be able to help it. He will never disappoint or abuse you. This is what people have done to you who are guided by Satan, who are themselves in demonic addiction. I don't care what their name is, what church position they have or had and what denomination they belong to. It was an abysmal sin that led you to be misinformed, to see disgusting examples and as a result, you no longer want to know anything about Jesus. They have slammed the door to eternity instead of opening it.
Remember the handwriting of Mr. Abominable!

And I apologize at this point to you for all those who set you a bad example by taking you away from God and his Son Jesus instead of bringing you to Jesus.

Please forgive us!

Do you know what Jesus says about these people, these "false guideposts"?

„One day Jesus said to his disciples,
"There will always be temptations to sin,
but what sorrow awaits the person who does the tempting!
It would be better to be thrown into the sea
with a millstone hung around your neck
than to cause one of these little ones to fall into sin. "
Luke 17 : 1 + 2
This applies to men and women equally,
who become guilty of you
and because of this you don't know Jesus or know Him wrong and sin.
Jesus, the Son of God, is alive and HE loves you and extends

78

His hands to you. He wants to save you and forgive you your sins. Sin is not primarily what you have done or not done, it is the sin of not believing in the name of Jesus.
(In the Gospel of John chapter 16, verse 9, there it is, if you want to read it)
And that stands between God and you and prevents you from going to heaven one day.

It is not enough to have heard about Jesus and then HE will do it. Jesus is waiting for your invitation, so He can save you. Everything necessary is already at hand. Maybe no one has ever told you this before. On the cross, Jesus has bought redemption, forgiveness of (your) sins and a complete restoration with His blood and life. You only have to claim it for yourself. Consciously say "yes - I need and I want". That's it!

Invite Jesus to come into your life, get to know Him and be your Lord.
You will see that Jesus is different than you might have been told.

A life without Jesus is boring, senseless, without a future. People without Jesus have no idea what freedom, peace, joy, enthusiasm, strength and suspense here on earth can have. And beyond that, a life in eternity with Jesus.

Where will you spend eternity? What if there is some truth to the life after death? You should have or get an answer to these existential questions of life. In our everyday life we take care of everything possible or impossible. But many fail to provide for eternity with the one who is responsible. JESUS! Jesus is the answer of God to our being lost. And one day you will not be able to escape this decision. You will stand before HIM, but then it is too late to make a decision, you must have decided everything already here on earth!
Decide now to live with Jesus and give your life to Jesus. Do

not wait for a later or better time. There is none. It is now that is important, because it can suddenly be too late. I have seen many accidental deaths that were torn out of life from one minute to the next and suddenly they stood before God the Creator and their Judge. They might have thought they still had time to answer this existential question.

No decision for Jesus? → Hasta la vista Buddy! Game over! Knocking-off time! Rien ne va plus! Too late! † ☹

I invite you to a new life with Jesus; to experience HIS love, power and forgiveness and that HE may take care of your needs and diseases.

Trust in Him!

You ask yourself how you should do this?

Just talk to Jesus!
You don't have to be changed before, become better or something. That's totally nonsense, that's religious rubbish. Just talk to Him in the situation and condition you are in right now.

If someone is to be rescued from the mud hole in which he is stuck, because otherwise it will swallow him, you don't say to him beforehand: "You can only be rescued when you have showered, are cleanly dressed and your hairstyle is right. It's nonsense. So is faith. As you are now - Jesus is waiting for you and will hear you. First the rescue – then the shower!

I once prayed with a woman - she was drunk as a skunk, but she wanted to accept Jesus. She had trouble praying the salvation prayer with me and I had trouble to understand her. But anyway - we prayed.
Two days later she was completely changed, she had experienced Jesus. Her life was getting back on track, she had become a Christian. It didn't matter to Jesus that she was

drunk. HE saw her need and her heart. And HE heard the prayer, even though the alcohol tried to prevent it. I am grateful to Jesus that I did not let myself be stopped from praying with her.

This is the Jesus of the Bible, my Jesus as I know and love him.
Invite him, receive Jesus. Believe and confess it.
The Bible says:

„But to all who believed him (Jesus)
and accepted him,
he gave the right (and authority)
to become children of God. "
John 1 : 12
(this scripture is so important, that's why I bring it here again and again)

„In fact, it says,
The message is very close at hand;
it is on your lips and in your heart.
And that message is the very message
about faith that we preach:
If you openly declare that Jesus is Lord
and believe in your heart
that God raised him from the dead,
you will be saved.
For it is by believing in your heart
that you are made right with God,
and it is by openly declaring your faith that you are saved.
As the Scriptures tell us:
Anyone who trusts in him will never be disgraced"
Romans 10 : 8 – 11

It's not difficult. But no one can make this decision for you. Not your parents, not your granny, certainly not any church, whatever its name is and whatever it has promised to you. Just you and Jesus. Only the two of you can make it clear.
Jesus will never force you, but you should think about it, because everything can quickly change.

Pray now, at the place where you have just read it, to Jesus and surrender your life into the hand of the most wonderful, loving, powerful and gracious Lord the world has ever seen or will ever see and you will experience Him ...

Jesus Christ

Prayer of salvation

If you want to get to know Jesus and you know that you need forgiveness and salvation, I invite you to pray the following prayer loudly, seriously and full of trust:

Lord Jesus Christ,
I believe and I confess that You are the Son of God
and that You came to earth to save ME.
You died at the cross for ME
and You took MY sins,
for ME to be free.
You have risen and You are alive.
I confess MY sins to You.
I pray that You would forgive and clean ME.
I receive You in MY life,
YOU are MY Saviour and Lord!

Holy Spirit,
please fill ME with the power of God,
so I grow in faith
and see more and more of Jesus.

Amen.

What's the next step?

Congratulations! Now You are a child of God! Welcome to the family of God!

You have taken a new path with Jesus at your side. The bible explains it as "new birth". This has absolutely nothing to do with "Reincarnation". You will not come back to earth in any life form. You are a new creature out of the Spirit of God. Not externally, but spiritually, something wonderful has happened.

> *„This means that anyone who belongs to Christ*
> *has become a new person.*
> *The old life is gone;*
> *a new life has begun! "*
> 2.Corinthians 5 : 17

You're on the winning team now. The devil's power is broken. Don't shake his hand again. He has no right in you anymore.

Now your new life in Jesus Christ shall grow and become strong.

Just as a newborn baby needs care, protection and support in learning, you need also in faith. You need people who know and follow Jesus. Who can show and explain to you how to live and talk with Jesus. By the way, this is called praying. Not necessarily pre-formulated prayers, but with free words what is on your heart.

Read in the Bible, it is best to start in the New Testament, for example in the Gospel of John, because there Jesus is described in a great way and what HE did and said. You can trust in Him and His word. You will see, it is more exciting than you think.

You need a living church where you feel at home. A church with people who love Jesus and are enthusiastic about Him and tell what HE just did again.

Where the Holy Spirit is free to do miracles. Where people tell how Jesus intervened actively and supernaturally. Have a look at their website to see if you can find reports of healings, interventions of God, answers to prayer or other miracles. If yes - take a look there, if no - well. Search for another one.

Seek a church where you and others are prayed for, where healing, deliverance and restoration are normal. Where you can use your talents and gifts and grow. There are more churches and groups than you think.

„For the Kingdom of God is not just a lot of talk;
it is living by God's power. "
1.Corinthians 4 : 20

„...and my (Apostle Paul) message
and my preaching were very plain.
Rather than using clever and persuasive speeches,
I relied only on the power of the Holy Spirit.
I did this so you would trust not in human wisdom
but in the power of God. "
1.Corinthians 2 : 4 + 5

Paul reminded the Christians that faith must stand on the visible connection between the clear word of God and the operative power. Not only clever words without visible demonstration of the power of God. If they want to make you believe that these things no longer exist today or that the Word of God, as it is written in the Bible, can no longer be seen in this way, beware of them. They deny God's power and you would not be able to grow and really experience Jesus.

Just Google for your city. Type it in:
"Jesus" - "Holy Spirit" - "Healing" - "Miracle" .

Then take a look at their websites, if there is life in it. Go and have a look and get an impression of the group and their meetings. You will find the right one. The Holy Spirit guides you.

But please look for a church or group. It is absolutely necessary for life. The Bible knows no Christians without a church. This would be spiritual death and the beginning of a lot of confusion. There are those who think they don't need a living church. Don't listen to them.

If you ever come to Bamberg/Germany, I would be happy to welcome you in the "Jesus Gemeinde Bamberg".
(www.jesus-gemeinde.de)
Please speak to me and let me know that you read my book.

Do you know that your life is now in the hand and care of Jesus? He now has your permission to fix things in your life and help you.

You will see!

I pray for you and for every reader of this book.

Jesus bless you!

Why prayer?

Slowly but surely we come to the question, what does prayer have to do with police?

Well, let me put it this way.

I have found that prayer changes things and gets things moving.
But I want to say the following.

Prayer is simply the conversation with God.

Not necessarily pre-formulated things, but with free words what is on your heart and what moves you, where you have questions or what you are excited and grateful about. Just like a child talks to its father.

That doesn't come with pre-formulated things that have been around for 500 years and talks to him like that.
Talking like you feel right now, honestly, full of trust, listening, taking time for it, thinking about it, ...

Prayer is not the "5 minutes a day" or before eating or going to bed. (if at all!) It's the whole day! Even when I experience something beautiful, I talk to Him and rejoice. If it is not so beautiful, I tell Him too. Prayer is conversation, conversation about God and the world and your life. HE is beside you all the time, talk to Jesus like a good friend.

God doesn't want to be just the stopgap. HE wants a relationship with you and me, to be involved in your and my life. He wants to talk to us, through His Word - the Bible, or even into our thoughts.

HE wants to give me ideas, solutions, warnings if something comes against me, HE is involved in my life. HE is my life! My one and only!

When I'm on patrol, HE is there. When things get dicey, HE is my security and peace, when I don't know what to say (should happen) HE gives me the right impulses. I have experienced this so often.

What do you say to parents, to whom you have to make it clear that their son has just thrown himself off a high-rise building and is now lying smashed on the ground?

This used to be the most difficult task on patrol. There were no emergency chaplains, no crisis intervention team. It was all you, the lonely Cop. They didn't teach you how to do it right either. We were simply informed by radio, to go there and inform them that he or she had died under the special circumstances. Come on!

In the case of the high-rise it was like this: we rang the doorbell, it was late in the evening, the man opened. We asked him if John was the son, "If so, we have something to tell you." The man said yes and we asked to come in. The woman was there too.

I mean, it's pretty clear that when the police suddenly ring late at night and say something about the son, that something is going on.

That was the first question from the mother: "Is something going on with John? Has something happened? Oh God! But nothing's happened!"

There's not much chitchat. There's no time for conversational diplomacy. They already suspect the right thing or the worst anyway, but hope that it does not come true.

So you replied gently: "We are sorry to inform you that John has died".

Hummy-- the bomb had gone off. Right into the middle of the family's life, their plans and dreams. Their happiness, or perhaps their problems, however well-hidden.

The man immediately collapsed on the couch with a weeping fit, the colleague took care of him, took him in his arms without a word and let him cry.

The woman reacted quite differently, she jumped up from her chair, grabbed the vacuum cleaner and started to vacuum the living room singing loudly. She kept singing: " John is fine, he will be home soon! John is fine, he will be home soon! Tralla-la!"

Ok, if you have done the delivery of death notices a few times, you know what's coming. The woman is about to collapse and go down. So I stayed by her side and waited. It looked like I was gonna help her vacuum. What I just saw with the woman was a frequently seen shock reaction, a repression, a not-being-true, a psychological or psychic filter function to let the just heard slowly seep into consciousness.

After about five minutes she dropped the vacuum cleaner without a word and began to fall over. But I was there and caught her. I put her on the couch with her husband, she cried bitterly.
After a few minutes they calmed down a bit.
I prayed in silence and asked God what I should do. HE gave me a thought and I put it into action.

I spoke to both of them about the peace of God that HE wants to give and asked them if I could pray for them. They allowed me to do so. I put my arms around both of them and asked God that He may now come with His peace to comfort these people. And indeed - they changed. They became calmer and calmer, the atmosphere in the room had changed. It had become brighter and more peaceful.

After a short time we could talk about what had happened and discuss all further steps. We still informed friends of them and waited until they came and took care of the parents of John.

Prayer had defused the situation.

Something similar often happened to me. Through prayer I got the wisdom and ideas in crisis situations what I should say and do.

Do you remember the beginning of the book, the armed criminal? The situation was also cleared up by prayer.

Again and again I noticed that prayer helped me in my work. I was able to handle complicated cases, I discovered crimes that others did not easily discover, "strange" things happened for my benefit in my job.

Once, for example, a man came into the department where I was on duty. He said " I want to turn myself in, I am a car thief, the stolen car is outside!"
That was a bam! At first I thought I couldn't hear right or he was pulling my leg.

But in front of the police station the car was really there and the car was actually stolen, advertised for a manhunt, the guy too. So I arrested him officially, well, he was already at the station, but everything must be correct. Then the man told me that he was actually on his way to Berlin (the Capital of

Germany, 400 kilometers away from Bamberg). He had already been driving for hours when, shortly before Bamberg, he kept getting the urgent thought, like an inner voice: "Go to the police in Bamberg and turn yourself in". In the end he did it, drove off the Autobahn and to me at the police station. I mean, he could have turned himself in to any other police station on his long drive, which was right next to the highway or something.

But no, to Bamberg - to me!

I handed him over to the special commission of the Criminal Investigation Department (CID) for further processing. As I later discovered, this was not his first stolen car; he cleared the air with my colleagues from the CID and confessed all what he had done.

Wow! Isn't it great?

It occurred to me that I had prayed for a successful work that day as usual. And that's what it was - a great success.

More and more experiences like these made me think more about the connection between prayer and police work.

Plan to pray more for your "things", expect a solution from Jesus. You can expect that! Write it down and date it. And then add the date of completion.

All a question of understanding authority

I mean, praying I did since childhood. Just like I was taught. I addressed everything to God and hoped that he would hear some of it. I was happy when something came true.

I the supplicant - HE the sovereign God, who does what HE wants without being seen in the cards.

So I grew up and heard over and over again that one should not dictate or demand anything from God. Nevertheless you could trust HIM - and I did because I knew- HE is good all the time.

But through the filling with the Holy Spirit (the baptism into the Holy Spirit) I got, it was around 1985 - 1986, opened to me a different access to the Word of God.

Much deeper, much more specific. More and more connections were revealed to me, Bible passages that I did not understand before were suddenly as clear as day. I had been a conscious Christian since 1970, but the baptism in the Holy Spirit made a huge difference.

If you are already a Christian, but have not yet experienced this baptism in the Holy Spirit, let me advise you: Let God give it to you. You will notice the difference, you will begin to speak in tongues that you yourself do not understand, that come directly from God and much more.
It is a mega strong experience. Don´t miss it.

I know that with this point I face opposition and counter-arguments, especially from some people. But sorry - I don't really care about that. I don't discuss doctrines, that leads nowhere. It only takes time, energy and after that nobody is happier. Everybody can believe as he sees it. That's also completely ok for me. Maybe some things are incomprehensible - but okay.

I have personally experienced the difference, Jesus convinced me by his word and his Holy Spirit.
I tell you with full conviction and passion: It is a huge difference that catapults your faith forward and upwards. I will not give it away for anything in the world! It has changed my whole life. Yeaaah!

My time and attention is dedicated to those who want to get to know Jesus, grow in faith and see and experience the glorious, miraculous dimension of Jesus. The Bible is full of this!

Back to prayer.
Through the Holy Spirit I suddenly realized a lot. HE is the Spirit of Revelation.

I am a child of God.
The almighty God is my Father in heaven.
HE is the KING OF KINGS.
I belong to HIS family.
I am a prince, in HIS image.
(It is clear to everybody,
Children of the king are princes and princesses)
I have the confidence of my Father in Heaven.
I am his ambassador, his representative.
I have received authority to perform HIS mission.
The resources of Heaven are waiting for me,
and many more revelations...

I started to deal with this knowledge and searched the Bible for it. I wanted, I had to know!

Here are just a few of the bible scriptures that brought my spiritual understanding and growth to the top.

"But to all who believed him (Jesus)
and accepted him,
he gave the right to become children of God. "
John 1 : 12
(one of my favourite scriptures, you noticed that already - right?)

"So we are Christ's ambassadors;
God is making his appeal through us.
We speak for Christ when we plead,
"Come back to God!"
2.Corinthians 5 : 20

"Jesus called his twelve disciples together
and gave them authority to cast out evil spirits
and to heal every kind of disease and illness. "
Matthew 10 : 1

"Go and announce to them
that the Kingdom of Heaven is near.
Heal the sick,
raise the dead,
cure those with leprosy,
and cast out demons.
Give as freely as you have received! "
Matthew 10 : 7 + 8

(Other Bible scriptures show that other disciples of Jesus also received this authority, not only the twelve apostles. e.g. Luke 10 : 1)

„ (Jesus) "I tell you the truth,
*whatever **you forbid** on earth*
***will be forbidden** in heaven,*
*and whatever **you permit** on earth*
***will be permitted** in heaven. "*
Matthew 18 : 18

another translation for the same scripture:

"Verily I say unto you:
*Whatever **you shall bind** on earth*
***shall be bound** in heaven,*
*and whatever **you shall loose** on earth*
***shall be loosed** in heaven. "*
(German translation – Luther 2017)

WOW!

The Bible verse from Matthew 10, like the others, wants to be
taken personally. If I take it personally for myself, it results in
my personal extended translation (in brackets), which reads
as follows:
(Feel free to put your name into the verse like me, but only if
you are a Christian!)

"And HE (Jesus) called Günther
and (Jesus) gave Günther power over the unclean spirits,
that he (Günther) cast them out
and heal all sickness and all disease."
Wow- what a mandate! What confidence!

("Jesus tells Günther personally")
But go, preach and speak:
(on my behalf, for me)
(And Günther speaks:)
The kingdom of heaven is at hand.
(And Günther...) ...Make the sick well,

wakes up the dead,
clean up lepers,
cast out demons.
It was given freely (to Günther)
so he (Günther) gave it freely to the people!"

That's first-class cream - isn't it? For too long I hadn't understood how I was meant to be. Hadn't implemented much of the Matthew 10 - verse. Oops!

The authority to act and the order were useless, unnoticed and therefore ineffective. And this is exactly the problem in Christianity today.
Today I see it everywhere we go. And we travel a lot. Into some nations and different churches. And everywhere the same problem.

Today there is so much social, political and eco-friendly preaching in churches, that we Christians forget what our primary task is.

Matthew 10!

We have distorted or even lost the focus.

We have put the main message of the gospel at the back of the list and thus consciously or unconsciously declared that it is not so important.

We made the headline into small print and are surprised at the result?

We are surprised that people are no longer interested in faith.

Sure, the other topics are also important and should also be addressed, but first the gospel of Jesus and salvation should

be preached and demonstrated.
That's pretty obvious. This is not meant theoretically, not figuratively or in any sense.

God says what He means and He means what He says!

He clearly defines what His will and His part is, and He clearly defines what He trustfully entrusts to His children, expecting them to know and do the Father's will.

Claro? Claro! ☺ !

Here you can write down what kind of sermon the churches and congregations bring at Christmas and Easter, Pentecost or other special days. Look in the newspaper or news. I wish you that you are not too shocked.

Accident series ended by prayer...

...and prevented further accidents.

One of the first experiences with the Authority was a prolonged series of traffic accidents. It suddenly rattled on and on. Injuries, extensive property damage, an enormous amount of paperwork for us.
It is already clear, accidents happen again and again, due to special circumstances, carelessness, but often also due to the carelessness and inconsiderateness of the drivers.

The consequences are serious. Almost everyone involved is in a situation of emergency. For the strangest reasons.

I had seen a woman standing next to her demolished car, crying heavily and sobbing. She was not even responsible for the accident, but the car belonged to her husband, it was his sanctuary. She kept saying, totally shocked, "He will kill me, He will kill me, I wrecked his car."

All arguments were not helping, as if: "You are not to blame", "It's not your fault, you can't help it, the other guy ran into you" or something similar. She couldn't be calmed down.
Only when we told her that we would go home with her to talk to the man and protect her, she calmed down a little.
Then we actually drove home with her and had to calm down a raging husband who was angry with his wife because she had crushed his "holy cow".
Mamma mia!

Another one, a young guy, caused a huge crash through excessive speed, with injured people and high property damage.

Instead of caring for the injured, he stood next to his tin bowl and fondled over the shattered lacquer again and again. "The varnish! The varnish! It's a special lacquer! What a disaster!"

Again, all reasonable arguments and explanations were of no use. We really had to shake him to get him out of his condition.

These were two extreme examples, but everyone else involved is also suddenly confronted with consequences. Consequences of a financial nature, of a physical-health nature, legal consequences, reduced mobility and so on.

So it is better that the accidents do not happen at all.

But as I said, it was crashing and crashing.

It was striking. Even the colleagues noticed. "It's like a jinx" and "That's not normal" were their strong statements.

And I realized this was another challenge for me. A man for special cases. And God showed me that I should do something here.
Faith in action, faith with the understanding of authority that I had gotten the last months.

And so I started to speak against the reasons.

"In the name of Jesus,
I bind the destructive forces
and I command the end of the series of accidents!"

My foundation was the Word of God and the revelation that I had the commission from God to do something positive here on earth and not simply accept the works of darkness.

Let me quote here a few small passages from my book "Acts 29", which I wrote in connection with authority and healings and deliverances. They seem to me here to be almost unchanged, significant and it also fits exactly to the police. I have added a few new lines.

(modified book excerpt beginning)
Jesus showed me some passages in the Bible that had to do with "speaking" and with an understanding of authority in faith.

Ok - the understanding of authority was not strange to me because of my professional training as a policeman and the related professional experience.

When I was in uniform, gave a 40-ton truck a stop sign, it followed the sign.
Not because I am so tall or scary, nor so beautiful or whatever, he simply stopped because he had learned to respect distinctive features and signs of authority. (uh - usually!) For example, he sees my uniform, my uniform cap, my patrol car ...

There is even a bible scripture that describes it in exactly the same way:

„When Jesus returned to Capernaum,
a Roman officer came and pleaded with him,
"Lord, my young servant lies in bed,
paralyzed and in terrible pain."
Jesus said, "I will come and heal him."
But the officer said,
"Lord, I am not worthy to have you come into my home.
Just say the word from where you are,
and my servant will be healed.
I know this because I am under the authority
of my superior officers,

and I have authority over my soldiers.
I only need to say,
'Go,' and they go, or 'Come,' and they come.
And if I say to my slaves,
'Do this,' they do it."
When Jesus heard this, he was amazed.
Turning to those who were following him, he said,
"I tell you the truth,
I haven't seen faith like this in all Israel!"
Matthew 8 : 5 – 10

,, Then Jesus said to the Roman officer, "Go back home.
Because you believed, it has happened."
And the young servant was healed that same hour."
Matthew 8 : 13

Wow - I got that. I suddenly found more scriptures and understood the combination.

,, After leaving the synagogue that day,
Jesus went to Simon's home,
where he found Simon's mother-in-law
very sick with a high fever.
"Please heal her," everyone begged.
Standing at her bedside,
he rebuked the fever, and it left her.
And she got up at once and prepared a meal for them."
Luke 4 : 38 – 39

,, I tell you the truth, you can say to this mountain,
'May you be lifted up and thrown into the sea,'
and it will happen.
But you must really believe it will happen
and have no doubt in your heart."
Mark 11 : 23

(end of book excerpt)

102

(Continuation of book excerpt)
The Word of God is absolutely true and trustworthy. It is powerful and mighty to overcome everything. It will exist for all eternity. It will be still in authority when the words of wise men, the words of any religion founders or others will no longer be valid. Why is it like this?

Because Jesus himself is the Word of God!
(end of book excerpt)

„In the beginning the Word already existed. The Word was with God, and the Word was God. ..."

„ ... So the Word became human
and made his home among us.
He was full of unfailing love and faithfulness.
And we have seen his glory,
the glory of the Father's one and only Son. "
John 1 : 1 + 14

„ Then I saw heaven opened,
and a white horse was standing there.
Its rider was named Faithful and True,
for he judges fairly and wages a righteous war.
His eyes were like flames of fire,
and on his head were many crowns.
A name was written on him
that no one understood except himself.
He wore a robe dipped in blood,
and his title was: the Word of God.
The armies of heaven,
dressed in the finest of pure white linen,
followed him on white horses.
From his mouth came a sharp sword
to strike down the nations.
He will rule them with an iron rod.
He will release the fierce wrath of God, the Almighty,
like juice flowing from a winepress.

On his robe at his thigh was written this title:
King of all kings and Lord of all lords. "
Revelation 19 : 11 - 16
(A description of Jesus in the book of Revelation)

(Continuation of book excerpt)
You can theorize it, tear it up, call it not true, question it, complicate it and whatever else I know. It won't change the truth. Jesus was - and is the Word of God and always will be. That is why you can trust in the Bible.

I have decided to trust the Word of God fully, even if I do not understand some things, cannot answer some questions or people come with arguments that sound good and right, but are contrary to the Word of God.
My mental condition does not decide about the correctness of the Word of God.
(end of book excerpt)

(book excerpt)
The point is that I had understood what the Word of God explicitly explains.

I received authority from Jesus to act in his name.

This means that I know what Jesus wants, what resources are available and what I may and may not do. That is understanding of authority and faith. Taking God at His word, because HE said and meant it. I act as a representative in the name and power of the one who has chosen, commissioned and equipped me.

I would like to illustrate it with my police profession.
The state has taken me into employment and trained me to ensure law and order on its behalf. He spends a lot of money and time to train me well before I am released on the streets. I get a police ID card that legitimizes me and identifies me as an authorized officer within the law. The state provides me

with everything I need to do. Uniform, gun, patrol car, computer, paper, my salary, training, and so on.

As long as I act within the authorization, the state stands fully with me and also legally represents me and my actions. He protects me.

All right? You got it? Yeees!

However, it would be a misunderstanding if, for example, in the case of a simple wrong parking car, I would call the Minister of the Interior and ask him to give a ticket to the cheeky driver. The Minister of the Interior (probably very enthusiastic) would answer me: "That's your job, I have authorized you for that."

The same is true in faith.
Jesus authorized us to do things in His name. To speak to the problems and diseases to change it.
(end of book excerpt)

So in this way - speak to the problem!

"In the name of Jesus,
I bind the destructive forces
and command the end of the series of accidents!"

And what do you think happened? There have been more accidents!

I don't believe this. I didn't expect this. I thought it would work.

Then I realized that I had some very strange thoughts.
"Stop praying like that, or it'll get worse!"
I see! So that's where the dog was buried. So that's where the

wind blew. Someone wanted to confuse me, snatch my guts, discourage me (you may guess 3 times where it came from).

I prayed to Jesus and asked what was going on. He also promptly gave me an answer.

With this prayer, or command, I attacked a bastion of the devil. And he didn't like that. He knew that if I would act according to the Word of God and believe accordingly, he would have no chance, he would have to leave the field.

Jesus encouraged me to continue to command and demand the end of the series. It was like the famous arm wrestling:
Press - hold against it - increase your own pressure - don't give up - don't let it go crazy - and win, slam the other one onto the table! Yes Sir!

So I continued to order, despite the fact that the number of accidents was increasing and the accidents were getting worse.

And then, after about a week or two, the accidents suddenly stopped. Like cut off. Nothing more. No more fender bender. I had him on the tabletop.

And don't stop now, of course. Keep going. Keep the field!

And so I prayed for peace and tranquility in my department.

In the other departments round me it was rattling around, the colleagues had a lot of work. When I was on duty, it was comparatively quiet in our section. Even the colleagues and employees noticed this at some point.

One day I came back from vacation and was greeted by an employee. "Thank God Gunther that you're back. Now it will be quiet again. It's always quieter when you're here."

That's right, on vacation I forgot to pray for my department. How careless of me. They noticed it right away. The workload increased immediately. ...but now it was going down again.

But it also struck me that there was a difference between praying and commanding, using authority or not.

It would be a lie to say that nothing ever happened again. But I noticed that less happened, series were finished, less work. Why it did not always have the "success" I wanted, I do not know yet. I think it's quite complex. But it was a remarkable beginning and I used it as often as possible.

In any case, this has already been a successful action to clean up accident statistics. Great.

But I must honestly admit that I often simply forgot to do it. Somehow Mr. Dark managed again and again to steal this procedure of prayer / command from my screen.

I'm sorry - Jesus and people out there, and of course I'm sorry for the work that went along with it.

Put it to the touch. When you read about a "series" in your newspaper, accidents, burglaries, etc., start believing, praying, commanding. Write here when you start it and when you see a change. You will be amazed!

"Bridge of Death" becomes a normal bridge

We were on a mission trip to Brazil a few years ago and a pastor friend of ours there told us that they have a high bridge near their town where people from all over the region come and throw themselves to death from the bridge.

We talked about it and I asked him what he or his church would do about it.

"Well, nothing, what are you going to do about it? That's just the way it is."

We realized that he and his church (and many churches we had met worldwide) had no idea of powerful prayer through authority and commanding / speaking.
We discussed it with him in a similar way as described here in the book. The "candlesticks" were opened for him. He had understood.

We drove out to the bridge and together we commanded this spirit of death to leave the place and get out of the region.

We encouraged our friend to teach his church and not to let up on practicing it.

After a few weeks, when we were back home, he wrote us a message that the suicides had stopped unexpectedly. Not one more. A series of years had come to an end.

All glory to Jesus for the effectiveness of his word!

Coincidence?

When I tell these examples, I often get the answer that it is all coincidence. They express that they believe that these things have ended without my "prayer actions" having contributed anything to it.

Well, it's interesting what people believe. In life, they believe fully head-oriented, science-obsessed and all that stuff. They believe in causation and effect, and "if nothing's there, then nothing's there".
And then they tell me about stopping for no reason.
Isn't that blatant? Come on!

Then I tell them first of all, just for fun, that I also believe it is coincidence. At first I irritate them a bit, but then I let the cat out of the bag.
The more I would pray for these things, the more coincidences would happen. Isn't that strange - or should I say "coincidence"?
If I do not pray, these coincidences do not happen. So I pray / command and expect the coincidence.

The other question is the definition of "coincidence".
If you ask Wikipedia (status 21.03.2018) there are a lot of definitions from different areas with different approaches.

A rather general definition in the whole set is:
"**Coincidence** is when no causal explanation can be given for a single event or the combination of several events. Causal explanations for events are primarily general laws or intentions of acting persons. The explanation for coincidence is **thus precisely the renunciation of a (causal) explanation.**"

So it was: "Where there's nothing, there's nothing." Or is it? There's simply no explanation. It is interesting that scientists of all stripes agree not to have an explanation for everything. Many theses, technical papers, theories etc. are only attempts at explanation. So the theory of evolution is also only an unproven explanation attempt, although it is sold to us as a proven fact. This is not true. It is the convulsive attempt of one who denies God to explain creation without the Creator. An endless, incomplete, pointless and actually stupid attempt.

If it would work like this, you could shoot half a ton of different metals, plastics, rubber and paint into space (assuming the stuff would already exist) and then wait a few million years and it would develop by itself, according to Darwin, a Mercedes, 450 SL in red metallic with all the bells and whistles - with WiFi!!!!
From the different metals an alloy is created by itself, from a lump of copper - by itself of course - finest wire fibres for cables, ...
Okay - all right?

So just because someone makes an attempt at explanation and wants to prove that it also works without the Creator, or has no explanation at all, it does not mean that someone in the background is not in control, pulling the strings. That there is not a spiritual reality behind our earthly existence.

The God of the Bible, the Father of our Lord Jesus Christ, is the Creator of all things. HE is the great engineer, the most brilliant and imaginative inventor the universe has ever seen - and will ever see.

„In the beginning God created
the heavens and the earth ...

...Then God said,
"Let lights appear in the sky
to separate the day from the night.
Let them be signs to mark the seasons, days, and years.
Let these lights in the sky shine down on the earth."
And that is what happened.
God made two great lights:
the larger one to govern the day,
and the smaller one to govern the night.
He also made the stars.
God set these lights in the sky to light the earth,
to govern the day and night,
and to separate the light from the darkness.
And God saw that it was good.
And evening passed and morning came,
marking the fourth day."
Genesis 1 : 1 + 14 - 19

„They traded the truth about God for a lie.
So they worshiped and served the things God created
instead of the Creator himself,
who is worthy of eternal praise! Amen. "
Romans 1 : 25

„To whom will you compare me? Who is my equal?"
asks the Holy One.
Look up into the heavens. Who created all the stars?
He brings them out like an army, one after another,
calling each by its name.
Because of his great power and incomparable strength,
not a single one is missing.
Isaiah 40 : 25 + 26

An English translation brings "the stars" more precisely to the point. German translations only call it the "Army". But it is not about soldiers. It's about the universe.

> *"So who will you compare me to?*
> *Who is equal to me?" says the Holy One.*
> *Look up toward the sky.*
> *Who created everything you see?*
> *The Lord causes **the stars** to come out at night one by one.*
> *He gives each one of them a name.*
> *His power and strength are great.*
> *So none of the stars is missing."*
> (New International Readers Version)

A Spanish translation also speaks in this scripture of the **innumerable masses of the stars**.

> *"¿Con quién, entonces, me compararéis vosotros?*
> *¿Quién es como yo?, dice el Santo.*
> *Alzad los ojos y mirad a los cielos:*
> *¿Quién ha creado todo esto?*
> *El que ordena **la multitud de estrellas** una por una,*
> *y llama a cada una por su nombre.*
> *¡Es tan grande su poder, y tan poderosa su fuerza,*
> *que no falta ninguna de ellas!"*
> (Nueva Versión International)

I want to confront you with a few scientific statistics, make you dizzy, challenge you and point out the greatness and genius of God - the Star Creator! When I read them so compactly, I became silent with awe and grateful. It made me realise all over again what a great Father I have in heaven.

Man needs some unit of measurement to somehow define and express his research and discoveries. So they calculated the so-called "light year" and defined its length.

In other words, the distance in kilometres that light travels in a period of one year.
So far so good - the result is gigantic!

About 9.5 trillion kilometres!
to be exact (here you go):
9,460,730,472,580.8 kilometres

You don't even run that on one heel. That's not just past Bamberg, Bristol or Yate → and than turn left! Come on boy!

That's a statement! An enormous distance! The beginning of God's dimensions! The dynamite that blows our imagination apart.

Okay, move on!

We live on Earth, (logical? → logical!) within the Milky Way. That's what our galaxy is normally called.
It needs a name, after all, so that the postman knows where to go. So it's the Milky Way! Please remember!

That's a whole bunch of stars, a certain spatial extent → and in fact the Milky Way has a diameter of approx.

(please note!)

100,000 light years
=
950,000 trillion kilometres

So manageable, more like a small galactic village.
Nothing special. Only a "village".

The nearest "neighbouring village" - sorry, neighbouring galaxy - is called "Andromeda". You know, because of the postman and all that stuff, like cards, letters, ...!

It is only a few kilometres from our galaxy boundary, a paltry, barely appreciable

2.3 million light years

I don't know if your calculator is still working, so many numbers in a row.

But don't give up, stay with me. Hold on to me. Check your seat belt! We're on the space shuttle. Star Wars and Starship Enterprise send their regards!

So far we've got "Milky Way" and "Andromeda" and now it's bang on!

So far, our good and motivated explorers have discovered

100 billion galaxies

discovered, mapped, photographed, given names and numbers, abbreviations, so that the postman can enter it into his sat nav.

The trend is upwards, because they have also discovered that the universe is still expanding.

WOOOOW!
Oooh - my - GOD!

And every single one of the 100 billion galaxies has

100 billion stars!

Now you're gobsmacked - aren't you?

Now it's time to sing the old familiar children's song:
"Do you know how many stars there are?..."
And the good thing is, now you really know how many. You can brag, pretend to be smart or just be amazed and praise God!

These are orders of magnitude where our brains drop out, most of them anyway. Hats off to the astronomers who can still do that.
And bear scientific witness to how big God is. How ingenious!

We get a careful and slow inkling of what "eternity" means. "Almighty God", "Limitless" and other statements in the Bible about God, his kingdom and the dimensions of faith.

This only in passing, so that you also know in whom you believe and better believe. JESUS!

And so back to earth, to the Word of God once again, as a crowning conclusion and reminder:

„To whom will you compare me? Who is my equal?"
asks the Holy One.
Look up into the heavens. Who created all the stars?
He brings them out like an army, one after another,
calling each by its name.
Because of his great power and incomparable strength,
not a single one is missing.
Isaiah 40 : 25 + 26

Boy, oh boy! What a God! What Majesty! What a Creator! What Power and Sovereignty!

Who knows all the stars by name and calls them into his path, and has also counted every hair on your head!

We're not talking about a "Wannabe", or "Mr. Important". We are talking about the King of all kings, the Lord of all lords, the creator of all things, even if some "Wannabe" here on earth covers his ears. They don't want to hear it because it's scratching their worldview.
It will change nothing - God is the creator!!!!!!

HE, who has the whole picture and will always have it, who knows the connections and loves man, the crown of creation, infinitely. He has proven this, that HE, after the fall of Adam and Eve, devised his Master Salvation Plan and brought Jesus into the ring.

Thank God for this!

„For this is how God loved the world:
He gave his one and only Son, (Jesus)
so that everyone who believes in him
will not perish but have eternal life.
God sent his Son into the world not to judge the world,
but to save the world through him.
"There is no judgment against anyone who believes in him.
But anyone who does not believe in him
has already been judged for not believing
in God's one and only Son. (Jesus Christ)"
John 3 : 16 – 18

„And now in these final days,
he has spoken to us through his Son.
God promised everything to the Son as an inheritance,
*and **through the Son he created the universe.***
The Son radiates God's own glory
and expresses the very character of God,
*and **he sustains everything***
by the mighty power of his command.
(even the universe, all the stars!!)
When he had cleansed us from our sins,
he sat down in the place of honour at the right hand
of the majestic God in heaven. "
Hebrews 1 : 2 + 3

„When I look at the night sky and see the work of your
fingers - the moon and the stars you set in place..."
Psalm 8 : 3

The God of the Bible is my Father in heaven, who loves me and cares for me. Who listens to me. Who knows me through and through. This is reassuring because I realize I can't trick Him and I don't have to give him a show. How reassuring.

So often we try with all our strength and effort to keep up our facade. It may work in front of people, but not in front of God. We can deceive or impress people, but not God.

Thank God for it!

„But the LORD said to Samuel,
"Don't judge by his appearance or height,
for I have rejected him.
The LORD doesn't see things the way you see them.
People judge by outward appearance,
but the LORD looks at the heart."
1.Samuel 16 : 7

And when I pray, "things fall to me".

So "coincidence" because of prayer.
"Falling to me" by God!
" Coincidence" due to the exercise of authority in faith, according to the word of God and in His name.

This is my explanation based on faith, the word of God, my experience in these things.

And I will have much more "coincidence"!

Here you can write down your "prayer coincidences".

Drunk "knifer" disarmed

Another example is an experience I had once on my nightshift. We had a big beer festival in the duty area at the time, with the usual side effects. Fights, property damage and a huge amount of drunks.

We were ordered on our patrol to go there, a drunk man threatening festival visitors with a knife. We drove up with several patrols from different sides because the location where he was, was known.

On our arrival we approached the scene of the incident at the same time with appropriate radio communication. The drunken " wannabe - Rambo" stood on a piece of grass with a big knife in his hand and shouted again and again loudly: "Come here, I'll stab you!

Around him, in a wide circle, a crowd of rubbernecks had gathered as usual. The drunk stood in the middle of the circle of people, screaming loudly and waving his knife.

We had to make sure that we got the situation under control before it really escalated.
The critical point in such cases is always when the "troublemaker", (the name is given to the person who initiates the police action, because he or she "disturbs" public safety and order and creates trouble,) sees the police.

In this case the police are the enemy who wants to harm him.

So a 2-man patrol approached from the front, openly visible, direct approach, because of law. We approached carefully from behind, concealed, in order to be able to start a surprise attack if necessary.

"This is the police!
Drop the knife!
Do not resist!

First direct, clear, offensive address.

The man reacts as expected, takes aim at my two colleagues, concentrates on them.

"Come and get me, I'll stab you!"

He waves and aims his knife in the direction of the two Cops, prancing up and down.

The circle in which he stands is quite large in radius, people respectfully keep their distance from the knife. It will be very difficult to stalk him unnoticed from behind, because there is a chance that we will still come into his circle of sight and he will notice us.
Then we would be quite unprotected against the knife. And that would not be good at all.

Shooting is out of the question because of the people, the danger of hitting uninvolved people is too great. And we don't have a real "self-defense" situation yet.

You can't really rely on our pepper spray when the guy is drunk or on drugs, but we would use it in any case.
In spite of the spectators, who might then also get something into the eyes.
So what to do in this dicey situation?

I pulled out my "spiritual weapon" and very quietly, not listening for anyone else, I said:

"In Jesus' name,
I bind the spirits of violence and threat!
I command to you: throw away the knife
and surrender without resistance!"

No one had heard. Not my colleague, not one of the people around, especially not the drunk.

But someone had heard it. This spirit of violence.
He had seen me coming, he knew me as a child of God. He hated me because I loved Jesus. He hoped that I had no idea of the power structure in the spiritual world. He hoped that I had no idea about spiritual authority.
And he was bitterly disappointed. **I had!**
And how I had! I had - with growing enthusiasm.
And I had the cheekiness to use that against him too.

It lasted maybe a minute or two. Then the drunken man suddenly stopped stiff as if someone had given him a huge knock.
He stared speechlessly, frozen in mid-sentence, into the air.

Then he dropped the knife as if he had hot iron in his hand. He raised his arms and shouted:

"I surrender! Please don't hurt me!"

Now the "big, dangerous" guy who had just spoken up like the "King" was crying like a little boy who had wet his pants. What a change, what a resounding success.
I've been in situations like this before. The command hit him like a grenade, like struck by lightning and had the desired effect.

But to be honest, I have to say that it has not always been successful. I do not know the reasons for this so far, but I will find out with the help of the Word of God. Because the Word of God is clear and unmistakable in this direction. It is a question of my faith, and that faith is upgradable and needs to be upgraded. I need to grow. There is no "enough" or "that´s it". There is always more. Clearly there is. I agree. Knowledge is fragmentary, so there's always room for improvement.

> *„Look, I* (Jesus, the victor over the devil)
> *have given you authority*
> *over all the power of the enemy,*
> *and you can walk among snakes and scorpions*
> *and crush them.*
> *Nothing will injure you.*
> *But don't rejoice because evil spirits obey you;*
> (It is not about a show,
> no matter how spectacular it may be)
> *rejoice because your names are registered in heaven."*
> (This is the main point of everything - eternal salvation)
> Luke 10 : 19 + 20

> *„Jesus called his twelve disciples together*
> *and gave them authority*
> *to cast out evil spirits*
> *and to heal every kind of disease and illness."*
> (I like it!)
> Matthew 10 : 1

Drug ring gets busted...

...as prayer breaks the iron Russian mentality

Another incident was also very exciting and ended with a great police success.

A few years ago a heroin drug ring was established in the German-Russian emigrant scene in my place of work. Suddenly they were there, not only supplying the young emigrants with heroin, but it also spilled over to German users. The thing was getting bigger and bigger and we as police couldn't reach the original drug ring. It was welded together so tightly. Nobody betrayed anything. They'd rather bite off their own tongues than say anything.
They used brutal violence to punish people who talked too much or accidentally said something. They set examples that had the desired effect. You know that from movies - but this was real.

The wall of silence was so thick and strong that nothing at all was or became known about the boss of this drug gang. Nothing at all. He was like a phantom.

This came up at a staff meeting and frustration spread among the investigators. There was no place to start, everything led to a dead end. Nothing for months - what a frustration.
All I could say at the meeting was: "Well, prayer helps."

I went with this request to our church, where we meet once a week (for 26 years now in the Jesus Gemeinde Bamberg) to pray. This evening is not about personal prayer requests, but about concerns from politics, society, necessities, catastrophes, worrying developments for Germany, the federal states, especially Bavaria (where we live and work), the city and district of Bamberg. But also for Europe and the nations of the world with their conflicts - and for my respective place of police work.

A comprehensive prayer programme, with ever new challenges.

Jesus explains to his disciples that this is their task. To work in, to become active, to become visible in this world. To use the opportunities of prayer to make harmful influences on this world and its inhabitants harmless. To stop the process of decay or not to let it arise at all.

Have a look:

(Jesus says:) „ *You* (the disciples of Jesus)
are the salt of the earth.
But what good is salt if it has lost its flavour?
Can you make it salty again?
It will be thrown out and trampled underfoot as worthless.
You are the light of the world
like a city on a hilltop that cannot be hidden.
No one lights a lamp and then puts it under a basket.
Instead, a lamp is placed on a stand,
where it gives light to everyone in the house.
In the same way, let your good deeds shine out for all to see,
so that everyone will praise your heavenly Father. “
Matthew 5 : 13 - 16

It is interesting that Jesus uses two different formulations here.

"You are the salt of the earth"
"You are the light of the world"

He speaks here to his followers, his disciples. They are meant, from them HE expects it. Jesus does not say "you will be" or "some of you", not even that they need theological training. A doctorate or something like that. That is all well and good, not wrong to have that. But the most important thing is to strive to know more about the Holy Spirit, the Word of God and Jesus.

The best way to get to know more of someone is to be with HIM, to listen to HIM, to ask questions and to go where HE goes. Watching Him do things, letting Him explain - and imitate Him. I personally love this kind of "learning by listening, watching and doing".

Jesus uses the Greek word "GEOS" for "earth" and the word "COSMOS" for "world".

"GEOS" means the geological aspect, the countries, the landscapes and regions, the nations.

"COSMOS" is also known as the term for universe, but also refers to all forms of orders, way of life, living environment.

And into the "GEOS" and "COSMOS" the Christians, that is to say the people who have consciously accepted Jesus as Lord, confessed their sins, were filled with the Holy Spirit and endeavoured to live according to the Word of God and its principles, are supposed to have an effect.
As a fact formulated by Jesus, a mission, a matter of course. As salt and light. Obviously the light at the "GEOS" is not very useful and in the reverse the salt is not very useful for the "COSMOS". Otherwise Jesus would have formulated it differently - Claro?

And prayer is a form of "becoming active".

In social disorder, hey man! - light must be put in, so that the causes of disorder become visible. Disorder does not change the "GEOS". The borders of Germany are not in danger or in

disintegration just because something is in disorder here.
After all, that's what the authorities are there for, to put things back in order. Do you remember what we said about it at the beginning of the book? I think so.

And such a Russian drug ring is 1000% a huge mess. And it was so dark around there that the authorities couldn't see anything.
Zero. Niente. Sıfır. Nada.何もない. Nothing. Nix.

OK - let's put some light into the dark soup.
How? We have already learned (if not yet - start to read this book again from the beginning ☺)

Exaaaaactly! Speak with authority and according to the Word of God. You are good! You're all in. Congratulations.

Now we're getting down to brass tacks. Victory awaits. We are only conquerors if we also overcome the obstacle. (That's the stupid thing about overcoming; something has to be overcome and is usually not easy, otherwise it would not be overcoming).

So I entered our Friday prayer with a minimal basic information, which was known from the daily newspaper, which had controlled the police for the purpose of witnesses or reasons of investigation. Faithful to my oath of office, not to betray official secrets and to be discreet.

But our "prayer group" knows when their leader comes with such an undefined request that something is really up. And they love to keep persisting in prayer and faith until that certain "something" falls out.

And so we started to speak light into the situation.

„All who do evil hate the light
and refuse to go near it
for fear their sins will be exposed."
John 3 : 20

„For once you were full of darkness;
(before we received Jesus),
but now you have light from the Lord.
So live as people of light!
For this light within you
produces only what is good and right and true.
Carefully determine what pleases the Lord.
Take no part in the worthless deeds of evil and darkness;
instead, expose them.
It is shameful even to talk about the things
that ungodly people do in secret.
But their evil intentions will be exposed
when the light shines on them,
for the light makes everything visible."
Ephesians 5 : 8 - 14a

Claro - ok? We prayed on Friday, the people took this request
home with them and together we continued our "prayer light
attack" on this darkness stronghold. (sounds almost like Star
Wars)

We were and are "Warriors of Light"

And now you know what happened?
Ok, ok, ok - I know you can guess the first time. You've been
reading attentively up to here. Yeah, you're right.
The Russian drug ring was blown up.

A few days after our prayer, it did not take long, one of the Russian gang members went to the police and against all expectations he revealed everything. So thoroughly, in fact, that everything came to the light.

Who the boss was, what names, addresses, cars, hiding places he had used. His suppliers and delivery routes, his helpers, henchmen, bank accounts, order books ...

It was like a lavish Christmas and Easter at the same time for our investigators. And we took them all out of circulation. Completely dried up the heroin ring. A lot of people went to prison. Hallelujah!

I always say the Holy Spirit is the best lead investigator and HE doesn't like drugs.

...Drug dealer disposed in Spain...
... the principle of prayer is valid worldwide

That the principle of powerful prayer is not my invention, my crazy idea, is shown by various reports. Remember the suicide bridge in Brazil.

The following report, which a friend and colleague from Spain told me in October 2017, confirms this.

Before I do, I want to explain how it came about. The Jesus Gemeinde Bamberg has its International Conference every year, at the end of October or beginning of November, depending on how the weekends and the holiday on November 1st (All Saints' Day) fall. It carries the name:

Natural - Supernatural
The restoration of the supernatural church

In these conferences we invite guest preachers who can speak on this topic and have practical experience.

The focus can be in one year on "healing" and the next year on "prayer" and so on.

The goal is to make participants aware of areas of the Bible that are forgotten or underexposed or misunderstood. They are encouraged to take a fresh look at this topic, to study the Word of God with the help of the Holy Spirit, to put it into practice and to make experiences with it.

The participants come from Germany (claro), various European countries, but also from South America, USA etc., with different congregational backgrounds, but mostly from the free church area.

131

Participation is free of charge, without written registration, further information can be found on the homepage of the church.

www.jesus-gemeinde.de/Konferenz.htm

And so it happened two years ago that a participant came from Spain and heard for the first time really something about resounding and powerful prayer. He had grown up rather religiously and did not know much about it yet. My joy was great when I heard that it was a colleague. The policemen of the world have something in common, the common mission, the common experience on the streets, the same happiness, the same suffering.

And so for the very first time, we had a good connection to each other, the same DNA.
And beyond that, even still stronger, we were united by faith in Jesus, our enthusiasm for salvation, mission and effectiveness in the world.
So doubly connected – you can´t beat that!

So here is his report from October 2017, as he reported it to me personally, but also publicly to the participants of the conference.

His name and country have been changed for his personal protection, let us call him Emilio, the city in Spain does not matter.
My remarks, additions are in brackets.

Report from Emilio:
"I was in Bamberg for the first time in 2016 at this conference and there I learned for the first time about the practical effect of prayer, the authority of a believer, the power of the Holy Spirit. The pastor of the church, himself a policeman for over 40 years, preached about it.

At first I could not believe that one could combine faith in Jesus and the police profession in this way. (remember that chapter?) I was really skeptical in the beginning.

We talked a lot and he told me many experiences from his police job. The results in his work, because of the combination with powerful prayer and perceived authority, inspired and interested me so much that I immediately tried it back home in Spain. I had learned something new.

Through the Holy Spirit and the now differently practiced prayer I immediately solved a long, hopeless case. (what and how that was, I don't remember - sorry.) This made my enthusiasm for Jesus, prayer and the practical impact in my job even more burning.
I am in a leading position in a drug squad as an investigator.

Three years ago, we got on to an international drug dealer in Spain and since this three years we have been investigating at full speed by every imaginable measure. But the guy was in deep water and he couldn't be stopped, we couldn`t identify or arrest him, the detectives and I were desperate.

I brought the case confidentially to my church, remembering the reports from Bamberg and my first own experiences, and together we prayed intensively for about two months for wisdom in the investigations, breakthroughs, clues and of course for the evidentially arrest of the dealer. We prayed and commanded light into the case and drew the dealer to light by "spirit and faith".

And then it happened. One day, an old man came to me and whispered something in my ear. I didn't know him and I never found out who he was.
It was an address and the description that a man matching the dealer's description had carried two large cartons into the house.

(Could this have been an angel? I think so!)

We did a fast access and caught and arrested the dealer with

30 kilos

in Words - please let it melt in your mouth:

Thi-r-ty Ki-lo-gramm

Hallelujah!!!!

He won't see the sun again in the next years.

What a success for Jesus, for me and for the whole investigation team.

Afterwards the other customers, small dealers and international contacts and suppliers were brought up and arrested.

> *„But when people keep on sinning,*
> *it shows that they belong to the devil,*
> *who has been sinning since the beginning.*
> ***But the Son of God came***
> ***to destroy the works of the devil.“***
> 1.John 3 : 8

„I (Jesus) tell you the truth,
anyone who believes in me
will do the same works I have done,
and even greater works,
because I am going to be with the Father.
You can ask for anything in my name,
and I will do it,
so that the Son can bring glory to the Father.
Yes, ask me for anything in my name, and I will do it!"
John 14 : 12 – 14

We were also able to arrest a second, long-searched dealer in the very act with 2 kg of cocaine (!) through prayer, confidence in the Word of God and the help of the Holy Spirit, exactly on the day I came to Bamberg for the 2017 conference. My colleagues called me and applauded the success, just as I arrived at the airport in Nuremberg."
End of report

All I can say is: Keep going, Emilio.
Grab them boy - through prayer!

Take your newspaper, write down where crime series are and the police are stuck, and start praying / speaking into it! Write the date when you start and then the date when it is done. You will be surprised!

Corruption controls the border...

...prayer & authority breaks through

I think here is a little report that has nothing directly to do with my police work, but still explains something about prayer, police and a great evil in many countries of the world.

The problem is called corruption.

In my opinion and in my experience there is a strong demonic spirit behind it, which works closely with poverty, violence and manipulation.

These four, it's not the "Fantastic Four", but the "Demonic Four", work closely together with "Mammon", who is practically the boss of this gang of thieves.

Jesus says about him in the gospel of Matthew:

*"No one can serve two **masters**.*
For you will hate one and love the other;
you will be devoted to one and despise the other.
You cannot serve both -
God and money (= Mammon)"
Matthew 6 : 24

Jesus is talking about two **masters** or **lords**. These are not two randomly chosen titles, they are positions of power in the spiritual world. Jesus calls him a "**Lord**." Not because he is so distinguished, so elegant, the "Lord in a smoking jacket" for whom Jesus has respect or appreciation; no, because it is a description of a spiritual position of power.
See how the apostle Paul, an old experienced "battleship", a general of God, takes this up and describes it. We will need this biblical passage later.

„For we are not fighting
against flesh-and-blood enemies,
but against evil rulers
and authorities of the unseen world,
against mighty powers
(= Lords, German Luther translation)
in this dark world,
and against evil spirits in the heavenly places. "
Ephesians 6 : 12

Paul describes here that it is not against men, but against demonic powers which manipulate, abuse and use men to bring their harmful and shameful works into the world.

Paul also uses the authority title "Lord" in this context. He does not speak about "demons", the foot soldiers of the "lords", the "mighty" and "powers".
This is practically the upper league of the dark powers. But don`t be afraid - Jesus defeated them on the cross. Super - isn't it?

So the "**Mammon**" makes his game:
He brings "**Violence**" in the offense on the left flank, "**Poverty**" on the right. The double forward runs against the societies of this world, in order to tear a gap for the offensive midfield, the "**Manipulation**" and "**Corruption**".
(I`m sorry for the example of a soccer game ☺)

They encourage people to abuse their power or position, which then goes down the whole social scale, to the point where the person has nothing more to manipulate and is the loser. Most of the time in this game they become criminals or they take their own lives.

The minority manages to keep the gate clean and fend off the attack. Thank God they're still around.

We know the situation, presidents and dictators get rich from billions of dollars in state assets, the small ones do it because the big ones are leading by example. A sense of injustice? - Nothing. They all do.

And from this follows unbridled corruption and violence. The history books, including the recent past, and the daily press are full of them.

Okay, I was on my way to Romania with a friend. He is the founder and director of a relief organization for Eastern Europe, primarily Romania. He works in Romania, in the Carpathians, together with a local pastor who is responsible for the distribution of the aid supplies with essential things and take them over on site.

Because we, the Jesus-Gemeinde wanted to support this, I went along to one of the aid transports in order to get a picture on the spot.

We drove to Romania with a converted coach (small part as a motor home, the rest of the storage space for the relief supplies - a registered special vehicle) and a big Van.

Shortly before the Hungarian-Romanian border a briefing stop.

The friend, let's call him Felix, explained to all the participants what would await us at the border and how we should behave.
Our papers and passports were in order, ready to hand and we listened to the expected scenario.

Felix explained that we would use the normal car lane, because we were not a truck and not a coach. There were special lanes for this, where the vehicles were jammed for miles. There was also a special lane, the VIP lane, which had to be kept clear, and there were high penalties for abuse.

At the border, when we enter Romania, an initially friendly customs officer would ask us for our papers, accept them and ask about our request. But he would not really be interested, because then the next question would be: "Coffee, cigarettes, chocolate!
In doing so, he would hold out his hand to show that he graciously wanted something of it and was willing to receive it in sufficient quantity.

Felix instructed us not to give anything, but also not to lie. We had coffee and chocolate as relief supplies for families and the children, but not for the border guards/customs officers.

Felix then said that if we didn't give anything, it could mean a longer waiting period at the border, possibly one or two days. Longer waiting times, he had already experienced that several times.

Here we go - the adventure began.

So we were pushed along in the column, forward towards Romania. Exit Hungary everything good, no problems.
Entry Romania, four or five lanes with barrier. In front of each lane a border guard / customs officer (there are different authorities, one police, the other customs).

From a distance we could already see the procedure during the check-in. Friendly conversation, then coffee packets, cigarettes or chocolate were handed out of the vehicle, the officer picked it up, went to his private car, which stood directly behind the barrier with open tailgate. The things were put inside, the passports stamped - have a good trip.

Most of the time at these dispatches were used for loading the "gifts" into the private car, the rest was nothing.

But the hammer was when a trunk was full, and that went pretty fast, this dispatch lane was closed, the border guard jumped into his car and dashed off. Sure - time is money, or rather coffee, cigarettes and chocolate. Besides, he was on duty and busy. They wanted to be back as soon as possible, in order not to leave too much to the other customs officers and to make more money.
And they did that all day long, 24 hours a day, in shifts. They had to run a shopping mall with all that stuff.

It's our turn! And just like in the movie, it reeled off just like Felix described it.

"Good afternoon, your papers please and why are you coming to Romania?" He took the passports and vehicle documents, put them in his pocket and asked for ... Guess?

"Coffee, cigarettes, chocolate?"

Felix answered truthfully that we were all non-smokers because we are Christians. We would have coffee and chocolate with us, but not for the customs officers, but for the needy in the Carpathians. And that we would not support corruption and would not give in to it.
Bang! The once greasy smile on the customs officer's face froze to ice and hate.
"Pull over - wait!" he barked at us.

We drove behind the turnpike, were now on Romanian territory, the customs officer went into an office with our papers, came back shortly afterwards without our papers, didn't even look at us and took up his work at the turnpike - uh, corruption tree again and - poof, the greasy smile was defrosted again.

We no longer existed for him.

We passed the hours of waiting by counting the customs cars, how often they drove away and who was the best. We had a "high score".

At some point I got bored and tired and decided to go to the office and talk to the man/woman in there. So practically from colleague to colleague.
And look - what surprise? Nobody in there! Abandoned! Our papers locked away without further processing! What a jerk!

So back out there with the others. Do what now? The big question!

"It all makes sense, God knows what he does, we pray for it. It's always like that." Felix said to me.

I got in my car and thought about it.

- ???
- ???
- ??

- what's the point? Where is the sense?
- that is randomness, abuse of power par excellence!
- they let us die of thirst on the long arm!
- that's time robbery!
- who do they think they are!!!!
- They probably don't know who we are?
- We are children of God on a charity tour!
- We act according to the word of God!

I tried to understand it
according to the word of God.
☹?☹?☹?☹?☹?☹?☹?☹

Slowly a holy anger rose in me and I began to attack these "powers" and "lords". It was time for a counterattack. Time to face them and show them our game. Because we are playing in the winning team of Jesus and the Holy Spirit is our coach.

So switch to „attack" and use what I had learned from my star-coach with the heavenly manual.

"In the name of Jesus,
Now I take authority over these evil spirits of corruption. I
bind you and command you now,
to return our papers and let us go!!!"

The boys must have been hard of hearing somehow! Nothing happened. So I continued in the form I just described.
I reminded them that they were defeated, that I had authority over them, that I was a child of God and that I was in charge here, not they.

Like I said, holy wrath.
There's something going on, you can see it in yourself.

There arises the "Lion of the tribe of Judah" - Jesus himself in you and roars like an earthquake, so that the walls shake. This is an image of the power and majesty of Jesus. The Lion!

„But one of the twenty-four elders said to me:
Stop weeping! Look, the Lion of the tribe of Judah,
the heir to David's throne, has won the victory!
He is worthy to open the scroll and its seven seals."
Revelations 5 : 5

I suddenly had such an image before my spiritual eyes. That was for me also the explanation why nothing had happened for a while.

My orders had blasted like a bomb into this bunch of self-confident, proud, selfish and arrogant corruption demons who were used to success. These orders had surprised, shocked, confused, dazzled, left them speechless.

"This little "Bamberger" pipsqueak dares to counterattack?
Dares to oppose us?
It's our stronghold here.
Here we do things our way.
Here we are the lords".

But then they sensed Jesus in me, the lion, the victorious power of the cross of Golgotha, had again their defeat of that time, almost 2000 years ago, before their eyes.

Horror spread, helplessness against this Jesus of Nazareth and his " Günther". The next round of spiritual arm wrestling had already begun. And they knew that they could not win, because the victory from the Cross of Golgotha was and is total and final. They saw their mighty black arms slowly sinking towards the tabletop by a trusting command from a simple follower of Jesus. All opposition was pointless.

The Word of God, the authority of the believer, the name of Jesus, the command not to submit to the black power, brought them to despair - and to lose!

Zack! The arm was on the tabletop. Once again, the name of Jesus was stronger than "Mr. Corruption."
Boom! That hit close to home!

As if from nowhere, the customs officer appeared, grim, angry, went into the office without a word. It almost seemed that some angel had him by the earlobe and was conducting him. He came back with our papers and passports, slammed them wordlessly into the vehicle and hissed: "Get lost!

144

He retired to his corruption post.
And we left!
There we go. ☺ ☺ ☺ ☺ ☺ ☺ ☺

Felix then said that this had taken a strange turn. I explained the prayer to him and the others with authority. They had never before experienced and known it in such a practical way.
The journey to the destination went without further incidents.

A few days before the return trip we came back to the subject. Felix said that on the journey home we could expect the same game again.
I felt the holy wrath coming up in me again, boldness and a new determination.

I told him, "Not like that! We are on a mission from the Lord Jesus! We're going to go one better! We're gonna drive through in the VIP lane without stopping, and they're gonna salute us snappy!"

I didn't know exactly why I was so bold and said these "prophetic words" at that moment.
Felix wasn´t completely convinced:

"Impossible!"

I called Andra from Romania at home in Bamberg, briefly described the situation and asked for prayer support from the church. They should stand together with me against these corruption spirits.

Then the drive home, at night. Border traffic was pretty heavy. All lanes full, traffic jam, exit with a long waiting.

But the VIP lane was free, closed off by red and white pylons. An officer watched the empty lane bored in his guard house.

At this point, it must be said that this track still dates back to the Eastern Bloc. It was always closed, was not allowed to be used, was withheld from political functionaries and their guests. It was a special lane that was hardly used at all.
Only for VIP's - Very Important Persons!

And that was us!
Children of God, Salt of the earth, Light of the world, Ambassadors in Christ's place, Saints, those called to the eternal kingdom, Kings and Priests, Children of the light, Co-heirs of grace and glory, and much more that the Bible knows and expresses in terms of attributes for people who have accepted Jesus.
Wow! YEEEEEEEES – WE are! **We are the real "VIP's.**"

So we boldly went into the special lane; I had prayed (my church too), faith was there, boldness grew more and more, to show these corruption demons this time too, to know the score, who is stronger. Namely Jesus!

"In Jesus' name
I order free passage without stopping
and with the official's salute!"

I now repeated in a spiritual command what I had recently told Felix.

The officer got spooked when he saw us. An old coach and a sprinter in the special lane, without a state escort vehicle. He awoke from his official twilight state.

VIPs on his trail? Nothing had been reported.

Who was it? Should foreigners dare to use this sacred, communist lane without the permission of the high comrades? It's unthinkable. It must be prevented with all possible force. Shooting? Alarm? Alert the border troops? Nuclear strike?

But since this monstrosity was not allowed in the face of the concentrated power of the Romanian border troops (1 man in crumpled uniform), it could not be. Where would one get there.

So there was only the second alternative, it must be VIP's!

So take a stand, pylons to the side, be friendly and wave through. Hand on the cap for the greeting - and Romania was behind us.

I don't think we even got the exit stamp. We had all the papers in our hands and we had them all ready, held them out to the open window. We should have stopped to get the stamp. But I can't remember exactly. I don't have my old passport anymore, otherwise I could have looked it up.

Even if we had stopped for a short time to stamp the passports, this would not have stopped the whole story and procedure. The facts would have remained the same. No traffic jam, no being held up, no time wasting. Using the VIP-lane with official salute.

It would have been interesting to take a look into the spiritual world in this situation.

How the whole thing went down there.
That would have been a movie! Steven Spielberg would have been jealous.

Do you heard about corruption in your neighborhood or city? Write it down and stark to pray against it.

A gang of burglars is caught...

...because prayer brings them into the light!

Another interesting story that I've experienced.

In a town where I was on duty, there was a gang of burglars. The number of burglaries in shops increased, the press reports grew and rattled the population. The police urgently needed clues to continue the investigation.

This helplessness in terms of investigations was also the subject of a police leadership briefing that I attended. The officer in charge explained that these burglars were so skilful that no traces could be found. Unfortunately, I have to dispense with details here, there should be no reason for imitation.

Ok, my dear reader, I know you are well behaved, one of the best, and would never use these details, but unfortunately the guys from "Picklock & Co" are not well behaved. Maybe they'll read my book. Or maybe they will steal a copy (because they are thieves). I don't want them to get any inspiration for their dirty business. They can read about Jesus, salvation, eternal life and being lost forever and about a change and a new life.

Yes - I pray for that!

So they broke in unrestrained, stole a bunch of stuff and left behind immense property damage and fear.
And as the German saying goes "the police your friend and helper"!

Well - in that case we could not help. We wanted to, we tried to, but so far... nope!! ☹☹☹

There's an old saying: "Be cleverer than the thief."
And to stick to popular wisdom, the burglar crew had made the "bill without the landlord". That is, in their calculation they left out one essential factor. Namely, that in the town of their mischief there was a Christian in the police force who had experience in successful prayer.

And so I brought the information, as it had been in the newspaper, once again compactly summarized, to the prayer evening of our church. Only the information controlled by the police press office. No police secrets. That is not even necessary.

Our boys and girls are hot and eager to pray specifically, to bring light into dark matters. Once they smell a rat, they won't give up until it's in the light and through the wall! You're my deputies, my heroes! My spiritual undercover agents.

The Bible says at one point in the book of Jeremiah that we should seek the best of the city.
The best thing for a city is when there is low to no crime rate, peace and quiet among the citizens. You don't need a theocracy that uses bestial violence, demonic rules, to frighten people so much that they don't make a peep. That is not freedom, that is not life. We can safely do without it.

That is not the will of the God of the Bible.

Rather, we need Christians who understand what their mission is, who use the tools and possibilities that God puts at their disposal. They are "salt" and salt powerful.

Look to this my friend:

„And work for the peace and prosperity of the city
where I sent you into exile.
Pray to the LORD for it,
for its welfare will determine your welfare.”
Jeremiah 29 : 7

„You are the salt of the earth.
But what good is salt if it has lost its flavour?
Can you make it salty again?
It will be thrown out
and trampled underfoot as worthless.“
Matthew 5 : 13

„I urge you, first of all, to pray for all people.
Ask God to help them;
intercede on their behalf,
and give thanks for them.
Pray this way for kings and all who are in authority
so that we can live peaceful and quiet lives
marked by godliness and dignity.
This is good and pleases God our Saviour,
who wants everyone to be saved
and to understand the truth.
For, There is (only) one God
and (only) one Mediator
who can reconcile God and humanity
(only) the man Christ Jesus.
He gave his life to purchase freedom for everyone.
This is the message God gave to the world
at just the right time.
1.Timothy 2 : 1 – 6

These three scriptures speak very clearly of our mission as Christians in the environment or city to which God has brought us. We have a mission, we have to pray to God (in the right way) for the city, for the people. We should not complain to him about how bad the world is, we should pray and make the world a better place. Salt, spice, stop the decay or not let it develop at all. That is our mission.

Some years ago we were in Brazil and served in a church with the Word of God and prayer for the people. Brazil, like many other countries, has a strong problem with corruption.
When we asked them how they would pray for their city and especially for the police, we got the answer: "Not at all, it is all occupied by the devil, these are enemies of good, our enemies".

Mamma Mia! We were terrified!
And yet they had policemen in their own church. Sure, they didn't have an easy standing in the police force. If they stood up against the corrupt system within the police force, they were mugged, transferred or killed, depending on how dangerous they became to the "self-service shop".

This was also confirmed to me by "non-believing" police officers when I was in a big Brazilian city for a presentation about the "Bavarian police and their tasks" and spoke in front of many Brazilian colleagues. Christians and Non-Christians.

We taught the churches we visited, among other things, the prayer strategies described in this book and how to understand them. If they would not start to pray and clean up "in the spirit", nothing would change.
For colleagues in the churches (and there were many!) I had prepared a short message, the "Double Authority". In it I explained to them that they had authority from the state, but also authority from the Kingdom of God. That would be a great thing. The power would raise to a higher power.

Not every Christian would have that - only believing policemen!

So no complaining, no moaning, praying!

And that's what we did to catch the burglar gang. In the manner described earlier.

> "In Jesus' name, we end this series,
> we bring the gangsters to light.
> It's quiet in the city again!"

I think we prayed like this for a week or two.

And then they had netted us. So not the net of the church, but the police. Full speed ahead, but they all did it. It's all useable in court. Stolen goods found, structures discovered and pursued, gangs smashed - locked up - done!

The prayer had once again brought the police an unexpected success.

> "Be cleverer than the thief and pray!"

Check your local police report. Take notes on which case you'll praying about and will crackle.

Saturday-Night-Fever...

and how to get rid of fever

Finally, a delicacy special.

In our duty area we had several discotheques, each with a high activity on the weekend. And the associated problems, which led to an increased caseload for the police.
Drunkards, heavy disputes, fights, hit-and-runs, disturbances of the peace, violations of youth protection laws, the list could be continued.
That's for sure. A disco is not a kindergarten choir.

But one disco took the cake. It was upside down. Sin City! Sodom and Gomorrah!
Police operations never end. Never-ending brawls. Never-ending this, never-ending that. It was horrible.

At 5 o'clock in the morning the drunk girls fought about a guy, who was allowed to take him home and get him into bed. Oh men! Nothing worse than drunk chicks, (this is not a macho discrimination formulation, no - this is a description of the condition) who dispute and fight. That's the lowest level of human existence.

For us as Cops unpredictable, because they spit and scratch like cats! (Oh - rhymes even)
They scream that your ears hurt. And poor boy - if you touch them too strong to separate them and calm them down. Then the spectators, the gawkers, the gapers, they'll come against you. Because you disturb their spectacle, their show, their vixen-wrestling. Just so that they don't make bets on which one of the Furies wins and wins the prize (the guy) and pulls it off.

The same disaster every weekend. The city authorities feel not able to do anything about it, that's all. The direct connection to the disco is not recognizable and therefore no further conditions can be made to the owner. (Hello?)
This view is reason for every Cop to get upset and helplessly shake his head.

The manager tries to get every budding argument out of the disco by his security staff, because outside he is no longer responsible for the disco.
Plausible – or?

And then the city governance allows and promotes "Children´s disco" so that the kids can have fun. I see it critically! The kids should get used to the real disco with all its garbage and scum. Oh Jesus!

No disco - no problems. A simple formula.

No beating for the last taxi, no beating for anything, no injured, no fight, no disturbance of the peace, no damage to cars by frustrated, drunken losers of the bed trophy, no public sex between, in or behind the parked cars (I could have shot a lot of porn movies) - with one sentence: Peace and quiet in the city!

I complained to God one day in prayer, reproaching him for not doing anything about it and so on.

You know what HE answered me? I was as surprised as you are now. I was almost keeled over.

" Günther, why do you reproach me? It's not my fault. I for my part have already done everything possible and necessary to remedy the situation. I brought my beloved Son Jesus to earth, He went to the cross to buy complete redemption, not only from sin, with His suffering, His obedience, His blood and His life. He also came to destroy the works of the devil. The restoration of the beginning, the dimension of the Garden of Eden here on earth. The restoration of the authority of the believers over all creation, in my name, on my behalf.

And my people have forgotten this! You have forgotten! I will not let Jesus be crucified a second time. It's your turn, your responsibility. You are the salt of the earth. So please don't complain, but act. I am with you, as promised."

I was flabbergasted. I didn't expect that. So I prayed for wisdom and guidance on what and how to do it.

Very quickly, I realized it was back to commanding.

And so I began:

> "In Jesus' name I take authority over this place,
> that's polluting the city.
> I'm drying up the finances,
> I'm locking the doors,
> I'll put an end to all this
> and the place should be clean.
> No more disco!"

It lasted about a couple of weeks. I kept ordering it. Then the big news in the office one day at the beginning of the shift.

The "mud hole" (name changed - claro) **has closed.**

The joy and surprise among the colleagues was great, some wanted to open a bottle of champagne, but of course we were not allowed to do that on duty. Nobody knew why it was suddenly closed. Everybody was asking themselves what would come in there next. It is often the case that a pub, disco or similar closes for various reasons, and opens again a few days later under a new name. The same old stinky cheese, just a new box.

I knew the disco owner and decided to ask.

He explained to me that the number of visitors had dropped drastically in the last few weeks, the operating costs were not coming in, let alone a profit. Since he had no other concept, no current successor, he had closed down.

What a surprise! He confirmed exactly the points I had prayed for.

Only the question of succession remained to be clarified. So I contacted the owner of the building and asked him about his plans. New disco or something? He refused and explained to me convinced that no disco or something like that would come into the building. He would have the building converted for shopping.

In fact the workers arrived a few weeks later and today it is a well-frequented, clean shopping centre with an inviting and friendly atmosphere. A benefit for the city.
There you go - it worked.

It has become a clean, trouble-free place that is good for the city. What a difference. What a relief for the police. We have enough other things to do. Thank you, Jesus. You are the best „City-Cleaner"

> *„And work for the peace and prosperity of the city*
> *where I sent you into exile.*
> *Pray to the LORD for it,*
> *for its welfare will determine your welfare."*
> Jeremiah 29 : 7

There you are!

Trust - look – whom...

... or the "spiritual Cop on patrol"

In the one drug example earlier, I had mentioned the bible verse about the salt and the light and explained something about it. Let us just continue a bit further in this context. You can also turn back again if you want.

Here's the spot again:

> *"You are the salt of the earth.*
> *But what good is salt if it has lost its flavour?*
> *Can you make it salty again?*
> *It will be thrown out and trampled underfoot as worthless.*
>
> *You are the light of the world*
> *like a city on a hilltop that cannot be hidden.*
> *No one lights a lamp and then puts it under a basket.*
> *Instead, a lamp is placed on a stand,*
> *where it gives light to everyone in the house.*
>
> *In the same way, let your good deeds*
> *shine out for all to see,*
> *so that everyone will praise your heavenly Father."*
> Matthew 5 : 13 - 16

Jesus, as I said, makes a basic statement about his followers:

Salt and light!

And HE says: "**You are,**"

HE **did not say**: "you could be", or "some of you might be..."
No! **"YOU ARE!!!!!!"**

It is the mission to his church, to his people here in the world. We should seek the best for the city for the good of all, in the sense and mission of God. And that's often very easy to find out.

For example, there are "businesses" that are legal on the outside, but not really good for the city and its people.

A gambling house, a casino for example. What's good about it?
It sucks people into their addiction, takes the money out of their pockets, makes them addicted to gambling, they lose house and garden, often their family too, often become criminals to get the necessary gambling money. It is hell on earth. A legal hell.
Admittedly, beautifully presented, music, private ambiance, subdued lighting, courteous waiters and waitresses - but it is hell for those who are trapped in it.

It's dismal to see when you walk into a gambling house at 4am to check up on things. Control. The risk of robbery decreases if the police show up at irregular hours.

Soft music, otherwise silence. Gamblers are scattered around the closed-off slot machines. Their reddened eyes are glued to the machine, imploring it to finally pour out the jackpot. Sweat on their foreheads and under their armpits, because they have already gambled too much without getting the main prize.

They are not responsive. Their hope and all attention is on the "winning machine"! But it is only for the operator. All the others are losers, addicts, junkies.

One operator once told me he only needed three (in words: THREE) frequent clients who would come regularly. Then all monthly operating costs would be covered. Every additional player is pure profit. I don't suppose he was lying to me.

I was shocked. I felt like crying. Poor Germany, poor world, poor people. They need deliverance through Jesus. HE can and wants to break the chains of gambling addiction. If you let Him help you.

In my time in the police I had a few suicides who killed themselves because of gambling debts, shame and hopelessness.
Destroyed, abandoned families with a huge mountain of debt. All legal - but wrong!
And more and more casinos and gambling houses are opening. Traps of the devil - legal - but diabolical. And the government is making a lot of money! ?

This is only one example of many. Everyone can see it as he wants. That is up to him. Everybody can go where he wants, it's his own choice. We live in a free country, everyone can, may and should have his own opinion and, constitutionally assured, say and represent it.

But I have been taught in over 40 years of police work at the grassroots level, partly through very terrible things and painful experiences, that not everything is great, even if it is legal. Many things I don't need, I don`t want any more, because I have looked behind the scenes. I got to know a lot of connections and helplessness, which are not in the police report or are not allowed to be published.

But it is nevertheless the responsibility of the police, under sometimes most difficult circumstances, to master their task, in order to grant the individual and society as much freedom and protection as possible and within the valid laws.

And Christians have the same task in this world. It's not about forced evangelism according to the old motto: "And if you won't be my brother, I'll smash your skull in!"

We had this too often, when unspeakable suffering came into the world in the name of "Jesus" or "God". That was not Jesus, that was not God, **on the contrary**, that was the mean old disguise artist, the chief illusionist. The destroyer, the oppressor, the liar → the devil!

Jesus came to destroy his works and entrusted his disciples with the enforcement of this basically settled matter.

Christians are therefore in a figurative sense, allow me this comparison, "spiritual police".

> *„But when people keep on sinning,*
> *it shows that they belong to the devil,*
> *who has been sinning since the beginning.*
> *But the Son of God*
> *came to destroy the works of the devil. "*
> 1.John 3 : 8

> *„I tell you the truth, (Jesus)*
> *anyone who believes in me*
> *will do the same works I have done,*
> *and even greater works,*
> *because I am going to be with the Father. "*
> John 14 : 12

Jesus came to destroy the works of the devil. On the cross he cried out "It is done!" This also included the victory over the devil and his works.
Then Jesus says that whoever believes in Him will do the same works as HE does, which for me personally means to bring the works of darkness to light and make them harmless. Through prayer.

I would like to make it clear here that it is not about damage to property, it is not about chasing after people who are involved in this or anything like that. It's about praying and using what Jesus gave us and taught us and what He expects from us.

I would like to show you another interesting passage from the Old Testament. It is great. It fits perfectly into the theme here. It would be worth an own book (who knows?).

„One day the leaders
of the town of Jericho visited Elisha.
We have a problem, my lord, they told him.
This town is located in pleasant surroundings,
as you can see.
But the water is bad, and the land is
unproductive (other translations: sterile)
Elisha said: Bring me a new bowl with salt in it.
So they brought it to him.
Then he went out to the spring
that supplied the town with water
and threw the salt into it.
And he said: This is what the LORD says:
I have purified this water.
It will no longer cause death or infertility.
And the water has remained pure ever since,
just as Elisha said.“
2.Kings 2 : 19 – 22

Wow!

I'm just going to pick out one aspect of many here.

The salt!

The prophet Elisha was acting in the name and on behalf of God. He came to a city that was basically good.

But it had a bad water source, the water made sterile.

And what does Elisha take, by the will of God, to cure this?

The salt!

That's right - I can see your thought coils rotating, your synapses are working at full speed. There was something! Synapses - make an effort! You can do it!
Bingo - synapse connection is established!

That's right! Matthew 5. You are the salt of the earth. Aha - so that's it.

> *„You are **the salt** of the earth.*
> *But what good is salt if it has lost its flavor?*
> *Can you make it salty again?*
> *It will be thrown out*
> *and trampled underfoot as worthless. "*
> Matthew 5 : 13

So the salt must go into the problem! Not the other way around. It is not the problem that comes to the salt when it no longer wants to be a problem, but the salt! Off to the problem and into the problem, Vamos – let´s go!
And then salt it all up. Show the problem what a good salt is! The natural purpose of salt is to salt, that's what it was created for. Not to stand on a shelf as a decoration in some pretty little jars.
For far too long, I have not understood that, I have not considered it relevant, I have been afraid, too cowardly or whatever else.

I have always wondered why the whole world tramples on the Christians, the churches, mockingly hostile. Doesn't want to know anything about Jesus. That the gospel has no broad acceptance in society. Here I had the sobering answer!

> *„You are the salt of the earth.*
> ***But what good is salt if it has lost its flavour?***
> *Can you make it salty again?*
> ***It will be thrown out***
> ***and trampled underfoot as worthless. "***
> Matthew 5 : 13

We wait for the problem to come to the salt.
For the problems in our cities to go away on their own.

We wonder why we Christians are being trampled on?
And God has shown us the solution through Elisha, centuries before Jesus.

We should face these problems, pray into them, speak into them, command into them, ask the Holy Spirit what strategy HE has and how we should implement it. Become active in the spiritual realm. Heal the rotten, deadly springs.

The experiences from this book are only a small insight into this area, I have experienced much more, but I don't want or I am not allowed to write about it here.
But it is the truth. All examples in this book are my experiences. 100%!

Supplement in 2019:
The prayer result with the disco " mud hole " was only the beginning of my "prayer journey". Together with our church we pray / speak / salt / command into the different "dead springs" in the city, the county, our nation.

And I tell you - more discos have closed, gambling houses have been closed, whorehouses have disappeared, sex shops have gone bankrupt and and and and ...

The closed shops have been transformed into other clean shops, supermarkets, gym, fantastic!

The Word of God and its principles are true, trustworthy and totally effective.

Where do you want to be salt? Hold on tight! Start getting salty!

Spiritual SWAT Team ...

... Motivated members wanted

Do you know the rotten wells in your city?
The "mud holes", places of prostitution, drug transfer points, fence locations, the public places where drunks, drug addicts, light-shy people meet and gather. Don't think that this happens by chance, there's a reason for it. These are spiritually " rotten wells " where they meet, they are almost magically attracted and don't even know why.

I encourage you, make a spiritual map of your city or region. Write down where these places are and start praying against them. Ask Jesus how you should proceed. You also can make it together with 2 or 3 other Christians. (Do you remember the scripture and the promise?)

We met so many pastors and leaders who really had no idea about their city and surroundings. But knew the genealogies of the Bible by heart.
Mamma mia!

Take your daily newspaper.
For me it is usually my morning read, my prayer card. My public information source of the rotten or good sources. Read the police report in the local section. And read it under the aspect just mentioned and you will make amazing discoveries. You will discover rotten wells, demonic, destructive structures, bad influences for your city. Developments, tendencies that are emerging.

You can and should also do the whole thing for your nation, for Europe. What political and social developments are on the horizon. Some of them later turn out to be rotten wells. That is our responsibility as Christians.

Begin to pray, seek out Christians with the same desire. Form a prayer circle, a "Prayer Task Force", a "spiritual SWAT team", a "spiritual special task force", just be strong salt.

Begin to study this subject from the Bible. Ask Jesus to give you revelation about it.

Start to take your first steps, use it, try it, and you will find God at your side. Write it down so that you can follow it.

Talk to your pastor, talk to the police in your church. Become active in prayer and authority.

Epilogue

I have told you a little bit of my personal police story.
41.7 years (according to official information in my retirement certificate).
And into my spiritual development, insights into spiritual things as I see them today, supernatural solutions to everyday police affairs.

41.7 years with Jesus in ministry
41.7 years of protection, I never really had to fight, never had to shoot a man
41.7 years of police work, from a little sergeant who had no idea about anything to a chief inspector in a leading position
41.7 years of miracles and experiences
41.7 years, which were totally fun, despite all the challenges
41.7 years! of which 38.7 years with Andra at my side, first as a girlfriend, then as my engaged and now for 39 years as my wife. Thank you for that. Thank you for your love, support, patience and your prayers. I love you so much.

Summarized in a small but meaningful sentence:

with Jesus on patrol!

You may have noticed, the whole thing is quite complex. Some questions remain unanswered for the moment. "Why didn't it work here and there? Or: What did I do wrong?"

It's not about magic, any magic stuff. It's about real life, about practically living faith in Jesus. It's about the salt in the soup, uh, in the spring.
And that you have to start doing it so that you can grow and get new insights. Not to start, because there are still open questions, is total rubbish.

There would be no inventions, no research, no progress, man would not even walk.

Did you know that it takes a baby over 1000 tries to walk? Standing up again and again, sitting down, up, on the bottom, which fortunately is well padded by nappies with inserts. All questions open and still tried. No idea about running, but driven by the inner certainty that it will work. Only those who overcome this challenge will become conquerors.

The world and also Christianity knows too many "Disbelievers". Too many "if" and "but", "Maybe" or "Maybe not". Those who then prefer to do nothing or try nothing. But let it seem important, let it make big, let the others know what's going on (or maybe rather where it stands).

Don't be like them! Don't give up - go forward with Jesus. Even if you don't understand everything. Suffer defeats. To keep on going, even though you often forget to pray and take your spiritual position. Jesus has forgiven me and HE will forgive you!

Hallelujah.

I encourage and ask you here for two things:

Number one:

You too, go on patrol with Jesus!

On a spiritual patrol for your city, for your country. For your family, your neighbourhood, for yourself. Be salty salt. Find the rotten springs that make the life of our cities unfruitful. Find the rotten eggs and pray them into the light. Give them proper salt. It's you, you have it, use it!

Number two:

Please pray constantly for the police!

For our police. Who are there for you, taking the rap. Even if you read the book in another country, pray for the police. Even if they are not as highly regarded and trusted in your country as they are here in Germany, pray for them more and more.

Pray for protection and preservation in their job, especially for the critical missions, pray when you hear that there are demonstrations coming up, possibly with riots.

Pray for the success of investigations and searches, so that those who think they can trample the law underfoot will be arrested. Pray for significant and probative evidence that can be used in court (this is what it is called when the evidence holds up in court, even if the lawyers try to tear it up).

Pray for more convinced Christians in the police force. Thank you.

And for the authorities who are there to promote good, to punish evil. That they are good and worthy servants of God. They can achieve a great deal if they take their task seriously and do not act and decide too laxly.

Pray for our country, for it is a good country! I love it! And you should love your country too. Do not scold about the conditions. Recognize them - and pray for them. In an unprecedented urgency. This is a serious time. Things are going badly all over the world. The good is being pushed more and more into a corner. Look at the junk that suddenly becomes law. Something's going wrong, because there's a lack of prayer.

Finally, these two biblical scriptures again, which have taken on a completely new significance for me.

(Paul writes a prayer instruction on behalf of God)

"I urge you, first of all,
to pray for all people.
Ask God to help them;
intercede on their behalf, and give thanks for them.
Pray this way for kings and all who are in authority
(today it's more the presidents/prime ministers)
so that we can live peaceful and quiet lives
marked by godliness and dignity.
This is good and pleases God our Saviour,
who wants everyone to be saved
and to understand the truth."
1.Timothy 2 : 1 – 4

"Everyone must submit to governing authorities.
For all authority comes from God,
and those in positions of authority
have been placed there by God.
So anyone who rebels against authority
is rebelling against what God has instituted,
and they will be punished.
For the authorities do not strike fear in people
who are doing right, but in those who are doing wrong.
Would you like to live without fear of the authorities?
Do what is right, and they will honour you.
The authorities are God's servants,
sent for your good.
But if you are doing wrong,
of course you should be afraid,
for they have the power to punish you.
They are God's servants,
sent for the very purpose of punishing
those who do what is wrong."
Romans 13 : 1 - 3

God bless you mightily!

I pray for you - the reader and hopefully also actor, of this book (here you may be an actor for once).

Write down your thoughts or questions on this topic, pray for them and ask Jesus for answers!

"with Jesus on patrol" international

We have many friends, including police colleagues in many countries around the world. Of course we talked about this topic of prayer, authority and resounding change.

They asked me to translate the book into their language, which I gladly did with the help of friends. That the blessing of the book will be even greater, more crooks will be caught, sources will become clean.

The international editions are also published by BOD-Verlag, available on the website of the Jesus Gemeinde Bamberg or simply online.

English: **... with JESUS on patrol!**

Spanish: **... en la patrulla con JESÚS!**

At the end of this book:
It is a small text that was once a flyer in our work years ago. Unfortunately I do not know who wrote it, it is circulated thousands of times on the Internet.

It is a respectful, loving bow
to one of the most difficult,
but most beautiful professions in the world:

the policeman.

When God created the policeman:

On the sixth day without rest, God set about creating policemen. An angel came along and said: "You've been working on this model for an unusually long time.

And God asked: "Did you see the criteria that the model has to meet?"

"A policeman must be able to run five kilometers through dark lanes, climb up walls and barriers, enter houses that the Minister of Health would not even look at, and all this, if possible, without wrinkling or soiling his uniform.

He has to spend the whole day in a civilian car in front of a suspect's house, at the same time scouting the neighbourhood for witnesses, investigating a crime scene the same night and appearing in court early the next morning to give his testimony.

He must be in top condition at all times, and that only with black coffee and half eaten meals. And he needs six pairs of hands."

The angel shook his head and said: "Six pairs of hands... - it's not possible."

"It is not the hands that cause me problems," said God, "it is the three pairs of eyes that a policeman must have.

"On a regular cop? Why that?" asked the angel.

God explained it. "A pair of eyes that can see through bulging trouser pockets before he asks if he can see what's inside (although he already knows and wishes he had taken another job).

A second pair of eyes on the side of his head, for his partner's safety.
And a pair here in the front, which can look at the injured person and make him say "Everything's gonna be all right, even though he knows it's not."

"God", said the angel and grabbed him by the sleeve, "Why don't you rest for a while, you can finish this model later."

"I can't do that, I've already created a pretty good model, it can persuade a 150 kilo drunk to get into the police car without any incidents, and it can feed a family of five with a moderate salary; I can't give up now."

The angel circled the policeman very slowly and looked at him closely, then he said: "Can this model think too?"

"But of course," God replied, "it can enumerate for you the facts of a thousand crimes, give you the list of traffic tickets during his sleep, arrest, investigate, find, and get a gangster off the street faster than the judges discuss whether or not it was justified, while the policeman is already arresting the next one.

And during all this, the policeman still keeps his sense of humour. Moreover, this model has an insanely good control over himself; it is able to investigate and secure crime scenes that look as if they have come from hell without batting an eyelid;
it can elicit a confession from a child abuser and still have its hatred under control,
it can comfort the families of victims and encourage them, even though the newspaper once again writes that criminals are not treated fairly.

Then the angel took a closer look at the policeman's face, he stroked his finger over the model's cheeks and said "You see God, there's a leak here. I told you you were overdoing it with this model."

"This is not a leak," God replied, "it's a tear."

"A tear? For what?" the angel wanted to know. "Well, for the pent-up emotion... for the injured comrades, for the insults he has to put up with, for the ingratitude and false accusations, for the frustration and anger, for loneliness, for pain and powerlessness, for the terrible things he sometimes sees. For the nightmares and the fear."

"You're a genius," said the angel.

God looked serious and said, "Angel, I didn't put the tear there."
(unknown author)

Acts 29

I mentioned in the book that I wrote my first book in 2015. I would like to show some excerpts here. The aim of the book is to trust in the power of Jesus and to expect that HE will do miracles according to His word, even today. If HE did it once, HE can and wants to do it again. If HE did it for someone else, HE can and will do it for you.

God's miracles are for all who reach out to him.

So here we go!

Günther Kunstmann

Acts 29

Signs and wonders -
they are still happening today!

The exciting journey into the dimension of God
Reports about the works of Jesus today

A motivating book of facts

Excerpt of the book:

It all started with hay fever

A dreadful discovery

You are around 30 years old, are thankful and happy that you have a strong, physical condition, you are making plans, you are ready to conquer the world and strong enough to pull out trees.

Who or whatever should be able to stop you?

And then my view of the world like this was completely turned upside down because of one incident:

Hay fever because of the grass pollen season!

The realization of this hit me like a ton of bricks, because I could not explain where it suddenly came from. I had never had an allergy before, I loved the scent of grass and hay, helped when the hay was reaped and I was feeling really good doing that. For me personally, spring time was one of the most beautiful times of the year.

Suddenly everything was different!

Burning, itching, swollen eyes; a scratching throat; a nose that kept running like a waterfall and no chance of healing. Medicine could only relieve it a bit.

So welcome to the club of the allergy sufferer!

This was a shattering prediction for my future.

Every year the time of the grass pollen season was horrific for me.

14 days' sick, spending time in a dark bedroom with the windows closed, eyes covered with Chamomile wet wipes – yeah great!)

Yearning for the pollen season to be over, so I could go out again. Into nature, back to my job, activities, friends and outings.

The mood at home with my wife was quite strained, tense, irritable during these 14 days – not what I had thought of as spring time.

You can surely imagine that in my head my thoughts were spinning around like in a merry-go-round. I knew plenty of people with various allergies and that they did not manage to get free from it, but had to get used to it their whole life.

Sometimes it was so bad that I wanted to live at the North Pole because the grass pollen didn't exist there. But then I realized that except for ice and snow nothing else existed there either! And so even that was no real alternative.

During this "time of suffering" this terrifying future was painted as clear as possible into my thoughts. I could twist and turn it, I did not see another solution other than to ask God to help me.

I knew: if anybody had a solution for my problem, then it was HIM!

"God is good" - uhm, excuse me?

As a child I grew up in a family with parents who frequently and joyfully went to a protestant independent church, and who loved Jesus Christ, God the Father and the Word of God with all their hearts. I went with them since my earliest childhood, it was absolutely normal for me to go to church and I happily grew up with it.

In early years (at the age of 13) I gave my life to Jesus. So prayers, promises of God and answered prayers were not strange to me. The church and faith were my usual surrounding. The Word of God gave me power and direction, especially during puberty. Till this day I am thankful to my parents, my brothers and sisters in faith and the church at that time for having taught me the "way of the LORD" and to have accompanied me. It helped me go through life quite stable.

Nevertheless, my way was not always straight and in my life I had done plenty of wrong things that made repentance, turning back and forgiveness necessary. Thank God, HE always forgave me and most of the people did too.

It was crystal-clear to me that God could heal.
Logical – HE was God and not just anyone. My conviction was that HE could do and not do whatever HE wanted to. Still, HE would be just in all these things. At least, that was a bit of consolation. This was how I had been taught. Of course I was praying for healing very intensively but it hardly changed anything. I thought "Well, then you will probably have to settle for that, maybe God does not want to heal you. Only others. It will be good for something somehow."

But I did not know for what it would be good for and I realized, that deep inside of me there was already a kind of inquiry to God - "and YOU are a good God?"
I did not want to question God but this little voice inside of me was not silenced.

This made me run into trouble because on the one hand I absolutely knew:

- God is good
- he loves me from the bottom of his heart
- he has good plans and intentions for my life
- I can always trust HIM
- he has given his son Jesus for me to be rescued
- the Bible is full of healing wonders and promises

182

- HE is almighty and very often we cannot understand him just with our brain
- the Word of God is for me and it is very practical
- …

but on the other hand I did not understand God and I wondered,
- what about the whole thing
- why me (I mean, I was his child)
- I was trusting HIM
- what did HE want to show or teach me by that
- why his Word did not work when I was praying
- and many more questions.

In the end I had to come to terms with it; I did it, had no solution, surrendered to my destiny – but I was not really happy with it.

An incredible realization

There are reports in the Bible you call the

Baptism into the Holy Spirit
or the
Infilling of the Holy Spirit

and which is available for all believers who have consciously invited and received Jesus as their Saviour and Messiah and who live with HIM.

It does not come automatically but should be asked or prayed for!

So let's look at three scriptures:

So if you sinful people know
how to give good gifts to your children,
how much more will your heavenly Father
give the Holy Spirit to those who ask him.
Luke 11:13

Then Peter and John laid their hands upon
these believers, and they received the Holy Spirit.
Acts 8:15

On the day of Pentecost all the believers were
meeting together in one place.
Suddenly, there was a sound from heaven
like the roaring of a mighty windstorm,
and it filled the house where
they were sitting.
Then, what looked like flames or tongues
of fire appeared and settled on each of them.
And everyone present was filled
with the Holy Spirit and
began speaking in other languages,
as the Holy Spirit gave them this ability.
Acts 2:1-4

One day I got to receive this experience and it changed everything!

I will not explain how exactly I came to be baptized in the Holy Spirit - how it happened and what the first effects in my life were. That is another story that I may tell you at another point in time.

In any case, the infilling of the Holy Spirit always has to do something with new realizations too. Things you could not see or did not know before, are suddenly clear and understandable. It was the same with me.

When the Spirit of truth comes,
he will guide you into all truth.
He will not speak on his own but will tell you
what he has heard. He will tell you about the future.
John 16:13

Suddenly I knew that the truths of the Word of God, the promises and statements about what Jesus has done and expensively bought at the cross for us – so also for me (!) - were available for me. Jesus had done it for me!
But I had no idea how to deal with that realization, let alone how to bring it into my life.

I started to pray and to ask Jesus to explain that to me, otherwise this realization would have been just for nothing! And HE did explain!

As an explanation I would like to mention that I did not start hearing voices or go into a trance somehow. But thoughts inside me recognized connections and understood what the Word of God expresses with certain scriptures, what it really means.

Sometimes there were these sudden thoughts I was wondering about, like "So where does this come from at once?"
Or it was like a dialogue on the inside. Very often it almost felt like suddenly I was right beside Jesus in a biblical report, experiencing everything as close as possible.
These thoughts and perceptions were connected with a big excitement, joy and expectation. Suddenly I knew what it meant to talk to God and also to get a reply.

I mean, I do know myself so I also know what and how I think. This kind of dialogue and these thoughts were new to me and were absolutely great. I knew this was God talking with me and inside me.

The infilling of the Holy Spirit had not really been taught in my church of the time. Speaking in other tongues, power effects, signs and wonders were known from the Bible (of course – it's written there in black and white) but there were plenty of people explaining why all these things were not for today or why it was not necessary. But there was also the occasional person I knew who had already had this experience with the Holy Spirit but they still seemed "exotic" in my eyes and a bit suspect.

So this experience with the Holy Spirit was the beginning of my journey in faith with Jesus, full of adventures, and it has changed my whole life.

First Steps

The first thing, God made clear to me, was as simple as:

"Have faith in my word and its power will be released!"

I said to HIM: "Since my earliest childhood I believed your word and have known a lot about it."
HE replied (in the described way): "Yes, you know a lot, still you do not really believe in most of the things but just say yes to everything. You think this is faith but it is not. Faith or to believe means trusting in the One, who once said it and act like it has already happened."

This was like a cold shower for me. And the same moment I knew: "HE is right!"

In a lot of situations, I did not act like God's Word wanted me to, I was a "Reichsbedenkenträger" (German, impossible to translate: a person who always doubts everything), I was

186

searching for reasons in his word, that justified my behaviour or doing nothing. I liked to take on so called faith statements such as "that's not for today" or "you can't know what God will do, you can't expect that from God" or "come on, you can't tell God what to do!", "better not get too extreme" and much more. Or I just had not got anything.

This new realization really put me in a fix. The only possible way was to commit that to Jesus and to ask him what to do.

Jesus showed me some scriptures in the Bible, which deal with "speaking" and the understanding of authority in faith.
End of excerpt!

Ok, how the story with the hay fever continued, you can read there in "Acts 29".
This much may be revealed, with the help of the Word of God, the power of the Holy Spirit and my active steps of faith, I got rid of hay fever - until today.
All glory be to Jesus!

There are also many personal reports about healings, releases of demonic things.

Here are a few small excerpts:

Excerpt:
Immune system gone crazy -
trying to repulse all the body muscles, the immune system fails against Jesus

Report:
On Sunday, 11th November 2012, a 47-year old man from our church was brought into hospital, as an emergency, in the early hours of the morning.
He could hardly move his body and was without any strength

in his limbs. He could not even raise his foot on his own, let alone hold a glass of water or open a bottle.

The doctors caring for him found out that his immune system was in chaos. It was suddenly fighting against his muscles. All his muscles were inflamed and because of that he was in unbearable pain. The doctors did not know the reasons.

Sunday morning his wife told us his critical situation in the service. In the early afternoon, Andra and I drove to the hospital to visit him. He confirmed the diagnosis of the doctors and that they had to wait for the latest examinations of the laboratory to try to find a possible treatment. But it would probably involve a strong cortisone treatment with an uncertainty concerning his future mobility.

So we laid our hands upon him, prayed for healing and commanded this sickness to leave in the name of Jesus. We proclaimed complete restoration and a normal functioning of the immune system.

After only about two minutes, strength came back to his limbs, so before our eyes he was able to hold a full bottle of mineral water again. He lifted his legs, bending them. Before prayer he had not been able to do that either.

Glory to God!
The pains decreased but he still was not that well. He improved over the next few hours.

One Sunday later, he joined the service again, and reported that the doctors had let him go because they could not find anything anymore.
The tests were absolutely normal. The doctors had no explanation for that.

Oh yes – and on Saturday he had already cut wood again. His strength had returned 100 %.

Jesus is so good and in HIS name there is power over the disease.

Bent hands working again
An older woman had arthritis in her hands so much so that she could not open her bent fingers anymore. The whole church knew the woman and helped her with her daily work because she could not do it anymore. Specifically, I spoke to this arthritis and commanded to immediately leave the woman in the Name of Jesus. The very same moment she got healed and could demonstrate it to the church. She held her hands up, stretching her fingers and moving them wildly.

Shopaholic
Some time ago a young woman came to my wife and I, admitting that she was a shopaholic. She could not resist, if she saw something nice in a magazine she had to buy or order it. It was the same when she was in a store. She knew that this was not normal, all of her money went out and she was not free. She terribly suffered under this condition.
Andra ordered freedom from this bondage in Jesus' Name. Immediately the woman felt a change. She went home and for the first time in many years she could throw away magazines and was set free from that moment.

Jesus is the absolute chain breaker!

For you have been called to live in freedom,
my brothers and sisters. ...
Galatians 5:13a

So Christ has truly set us free!
Now make sure that you stay free, and don't get tied up again
in slavery to the law.
Galatians 5:1

Here we have it in black and white. We should be free and Jesus has set us free. The preconditions are given, come and get this freedom from Jesus. People experience it every day – so why not you as well!

Here we have it in black and white. We should be free and Jesus has set us free. The preconditions are given, come and get this freedom from Jesus. People experience it every day – so why not you as well!

...This book describes in an understandable way how Jesus does miracles in the lives of people. And still does so today. Amazing reports, which inspire and motivate, make people wonder and hope and rekindle their own faith in Jesus. Questions, arguments, obstacles for the supernatural work of God are illuminated as well as the simple knowledge and statement:
Nothing is impossible for Jesus.

Personal experiences and life changes will encourage us to see our own situations in a new light and to tackle and change them in the power of Jesus.
end of excerpt from the book

The book simply shows that miracles have not stopped but are still happening. Also for you! Study Jesus and His Word and you will find out that He has done so many miracles, healed all possible and impossible ways. No illness, no demonic power was safe from Him. HE has shown the love of God in action.

The book "Acts 29" has 136 pages
and is priced at 9.99 Euro.
It is published by BOD-Verlag Norderstedt / Germany
ISBN number: 9783741250552

It is available online in the BOD book shop
(https://www.bod.de/buchshop/catalogsearch/result/?q=acts+29)

or via other online dealers, e.g. AMAZON, …

This also is available internationally:

German: „Apostelgeschichte 29"
                 ISBN: 9783738636468

Spanish: "Hechos 29"
                 ISBN: 9783746067537

Portugues: "Atos 29"
                 ISBN: 9783744817240

Perhaps you would like to give some friends a copy in their
own language?

Have fun and many good insights while reading!

Here we gooooooooo →

And now it only remains for me to say:

Let's rock the spiritual forces by prayer.

The world and your city are waiting for you!

You will experience something incredible,
that you can tell your grandchildren one day.

Start salting!

I pray for you dear reader, that you will be totally touched
and encouraged by Jesus and that you will experience
amazing experiences and miracles.

**Be blessed
in the name of Jesus Christ**

**...
your friends and partners
Günther & Andra**

© Günther Kunstmann
Bamberg, February 2020

MIX
Papier aus verantwortungsvollen Quellen
Paper from responsible sources
FSC® C105338
FSC
www.fsc.org